The 10 Best Years of
BASEBALL
An Informal History of the Fifties
Harold Rosenthal

Phillies   *Orioles*

Spence

"I always remember Chuck Dressen — "you guys stay close to the eighth, I'll think of something."

Gary

VNR VAN NOSTRAND REINHOLD COMPANY
NEW YORK CINCINNATI TORONTO LONDON MELBOURNE

Library of Congress Cataloging in Publication Data

Rosenthal, Harold.
    The 10 best years of baseball.

    1. Baseball—United States—History.   I. Title.
GV863.A1R63   796.357'0973   80–53040
ISBN 0–442–27063–1

To the Baseball Writers Association of America
And the tradition of Grantland Rice

First published in paperback in 1981
Copyright © 1979 by Harold Rosenthal
Library of Congress Catalog Card Number
80–53040
ISBN 0–442–27063–1

Van Nostrand Reinhold Company
A division of Litton Educational Publishing, Inc.
135 West 50th Street, New York, NY 10020

Van Nostrand Reinhold Ltd.
1410 Birchmount Road, Scarborough,
Ontario M1P 2E7

Van Nostrand Reinhold Australia Pty. Ltd.
17 Queen Street, Mitcham, Victoria 3132

Van Nostrand Reinhold Company Ltd.
Molly Millars Lane, Wokingham,
Berkshire, England RG11 2PY

Cloth edition published 1979 by Contemporary
Books, Inc.

16 15 14 13 12 11 10 9 8 7 6 5 4 3 2 1

Contents

Preface

THERE IS AMPLE MATERIAL in baseball's fabulous fifties for not one book but a dozen. Public interest ran high; TV's influence and manipulation was low, if any. The lunatic owner had not yet appeared. Bill Veeck was around making waves but the dumbest of the overlords was instinctively aware of the difference between a nut and a maverick.

The fifties ball player was a celebrity because of his actions on the field, not because of his corporate activities or his ability to smirk through a commercial. The few times a ball player sought a lawyer's advice (There were a lot fewer lawyers in the fifties, too.) it seldom had anything to do with a playing contract. Players usually handled their own contracts.

Lawyers were for more delicate proceedings like divorces or paternity cases. Still remembered is a key owner in the fifties, law-trained, who defended one of the numbskulls whose fastball had kept him around even though his personality dictated he be shown out the door. A young lady had come asking, "What about the baby?" and the ball player had provided the standard "Who, me?" reply. The owner did everything but imply that he had been among those who had dated the lady himself. He further assured this harassed but upstanding young man that the entire resources of the organization were at his complete disposal.

Try that on some owner today, especially if he has been pushed around all too recently by some twenty-five-year-old agent on behalf of a client seeking a five-year no-cut contract at $352,000 but who was willing to settle for $325,000. Gad man, he'd gladly let the fellow hang by the appurtenance that had led him into the jam in the first place.

Baseball is a lot like the Atlantic Ocean, the Pacific, or the Gulf of Mexico. It was there when we looked for the first time and it'll be there when we have that last look. And the same will hold true for baseball fans five hundred years hence.

The game, like some mighty body of water, is calm and stormy by turns. It can engulf completely such nit-witticisms as designated hitters, six o'clock World Series starts, cold hot dogs, and warm beer. Everything soon becomes a part of the whole, and the ripples disappear quickly.

The identity of the person who invented baseball is lost in antiquity. (It certainly isn't our old friend, General Abner Doubleday, or he'd be in the Hall of Fame up in Cooperstown along with Tinker, Evers, and Chance, or at least with Henry Chadwick, the Civil War sports writer who invented the box score, wouldn't he?)

Also missing is the person who viewed a few days of intensive anti-trust hearings and haggling before one of those broad-bottomed Congressional committees back in the fifties whose objective was to try to determine whether baseball was a sport or a business. "A business?" he snorted. "If it was, we'd all be broke in a year."

The fifties were a time of high excitement in baseball. The hope is that some of it might be conveyed in the following pages.

1

More than Just Clipping Coupons

BASEBALL BEGAN the fifties with sixteen teams, the same number as it had when the American League joined the National at the start of the century. Expansion was still a decade away. There were sixteen teams when the fifties finished but there was a sharp difference.

The map of the game had been altered dramatically. Instead of being confined roughly to an area east of the Mississippi and north of the Mason-Dixon Line, it had gone Coast-to-Coast. The list of two-team cities (New York, Boston, Chicago, Philadelphia and St. Louis) had been cut to include only Chicago. Obviously the game was on the move, although the burgeoning of the roster to more than two-dozen was still up the road a bit.

New York lost two of its three teams when Walter O'Malley moved Brooklyn to Los Angeles and Horace Stoneham hustled after him, yanking the Giants out of the moribund Polo Grounds and setting up shop in San Francisco. Both played in temporary facilities before moving into new arenas. The Dodgers occupied a weird-shaped (for baseball) Los Angeles Memorial Coliseum; the Giants played in the old Seals Stadium where the Pacific Coast League's club had been.

The Boston Braves quit the Athens of America only five years after winning the National League flag. Attendance had dipped from almost a million and a half to a quarter-million and Milwaukee beckoned with a brand-new stadium and a super deal.

Philadelphia lost the Athletics, which had been owned by the Mack family since the formation of the American League. Age had taken its toll of the patriarchal Connie Mack and his descendants weren't up to the task of matching up to modern-day ball. They sold out to a group from Chicago, headed up by Arnold Johnson, a friend of Del Webb, of the Yankees and when the A's showed up in Kansas City, baseball had crossed the wide Mississippi just like Hernando De Soto a few centuries earlier. The airplane had taken the edge off distances and was to help even more when the jump was made to the West Coast.

St. Louis lost the Browns and in the process a lot of owners got even with Bill Veeck. As owner along with the DeWitts, Bill and Charley, Veeck was frequently able to move around Sportsman's Park and shake hands with everyone who came to see his club play that particular afternoon or evening. The other American League owners granted permission for the sale to Baltimore with one stipulation; Veeck was out.

Squirming on a financial hook, baseball's No. 1 gadfly had no recourse except to accept first the dictum and then the money which would pay off his creditors. Muttering, he went underground, occasionally raising his burr-head for a view of the landscape.

In the last year of the decade the chronically strapped Comiskey family, descendants of old Charlie, whose tight-fisted attitude toward his players permitted the gamblers to have entry to his club and precipitate what was to prove the only crooked World Series, the 1919 Black Sox scandal, couldn't cut it any more in Chicago. A group headed by Hank Greenberg and Veeck bought them out and promptly won a pennant.

At his World Series party in Chicago, Veeck gave some of his old foes heartburn with a Lucullan splash that included vintage grape pumping through table fountains. He did this partly out of his love of a big party lasting into the morning hours and partly to show up the Dodgers, who had blinked the lights at 10:30 p.m. at their party in Los Angeles.

Greenberg had been a superstar at Detroit in the thirties and forties, plus the game's first $100,000 ball player with the Pirates in 1946. He was a plugging, highly successful business-man, slightly remarkable because his only training had been in baseball.

Veeck was a latter-day P. T. Barnum, seemingly more inter-ested in pulling off some outrageous stunt that would cause tongues to wag (midgets at the plate, rockets in the scoreboard) than anything else. He was constantly seeking the noisy approval of his critics, who included everyone from the beer-guzzlers in the bleachers to the sports mavens in their spurious ivory tow-ers.

Veeck made no particular big deal of it, but he could also judge baseball talent. Baseball blood coursed through his body and three limbs. (One leg had been left on Guadalcanal. Bill spent the next twenty years having various medical people whittle it shorter and shorter.)

Veeck's father, William Sr., had been moved into the role of president of the Chicago Cubs when Willie was three. Daddy got William Wrigley's practically undivided attention via his column in the *Chicago American* in which he announced almost daily that he could do a better job than the incumbent. A generation later another Chicago newsman, Jimmy Gallagher, pulled the same stunt on Wrigley's son, Philip K.

Gallagher was somewhat less successful than Veeck's old man. One of Larry MacPhail's great coups in Brooklyn was to keep Gallagher up into the morning and trade a couple of pedestrian players (Johnny Hudson and Charley Gilbert, if names are necessary) for Hall of Famer Billy Herman.

Veeck was a boy baseball entrepreneur and he was equally as smart as his father. Junior was running the Milwaukee club in the American Association just prior to answering his country's call. When Charley Grimm was called up to run the Cubs in the early part of '44 Veeck got on the phone to a wise-ass with big ears and sharp tongue who had been somewhat less than successful for the previous five years with the lowly Boston Braves. His pick, Casey Stengel, promptly won the American Association pennant for him.

After the war Veeck hooked up with Hank Greenberg to run the Cleveland Indians. They not only won the 1948 pennant, setting an attendance record along with it, but beat the Braves in the World Series. Player-manager Lou Boudreau was of singular help in this project. He hit .355 in the regular season, whacked four doubles in the Series. Good managers appreciate good hitters and Lou did everything but write himself a fan letter.

Veeck and Greenberg sold out and Veeck took his end and invested it in what looked like a good deal in St. Louis. A local coal and ice monger was trying to get rid of the Browns and it looked like an attractive investment. The ball park real estate went along with it. The Cardinals, who by now were the bigger attraction with players like Musial, Marty Marion and Enos Slaughter, were just rent-payers.

But times and attitudes had changed after World War II, along with players' salaries and club expenses. No longer could you put two players into a first-class hotel room for four dollars a night and feed them on five dollars a day meal money. And gone were the days when the front office worked its personnel seventy hours a week and paid them off in the dark, throwing in a couple of passes for the garageman for the Sunday doubleheader. Not just in St. Louis but everywhere else.

St. Louis, like most of the other two-team cities, simply couldn't support two clubs. The Cardinals, manifestly superior, were going to remain that way, on the field and at the gate.

Veeck struggled a while in St. Louis and got loads of publicity with his stunts. There was the midget at the plate; there was Zack Taylor, the manager in a rocking chair while the fans were asked to manage via placards ("Bunt," "Hit Away"); there was the ageless Satchel Paige, who had been brought into organized ball by Veeck in 1948, back for another trip over the course; and much more. Veeck drew lots of national publicity but the locals just read all about it in the *Post-Dispatch* and *Globe Democrat* and saved their nickels to see the Cardinals when they came off the road.

Veeck also continued his needling the owners who were less brainy than he, and he had plenty of targets. Beaten in the "Oh, he said that, did he?" department they licked their wounds and bided their time. Gladly they'd have chipped in on a contract for someone to break his remaining leg.

Case in point. Veeck could see, probably better than most, that the electronic medium was going to play an increasingly important role in the financial end of baseball. It was only the beginning though and Veeck wanted to make a point. He asked the Yankees and everyone else for a share of their radio and TV revenue. His reasoning was that two teams were required to play a game, and the Browns certainly were contributing to the activity.

Maybe Veeck would have had a fairly sympathetic audience in some cities like Philadelphia and Washington where radio amounted to nickels and dimes, but New York was the No. 1 market. George Weiss, the Yankee general manager, looked dimly on the suggestion and said he thought the guy was some kind of a Communist. Didn't think much either of Veeck's offer that he'd be glad to split his own revenue in St. Louis with the Yankees.

Weiss squirmed as Veeck slipped the needle in but still managed to maintain a firm grasp on his dignity—and the Yankee receipts. "When you were doing more than two-million people in Cleveland," he choked out, "why didn't you offer to split your radio with everyone else? Why all of a sudden now?"

Veeck's reply was, "Circumstances alter cases."

The intention here is not to re-write a history of Bill Veeck. He's already done that in several books including *Veeck, as in*

Wreck, The Hustler's Handbook and *Thirty Tons a Day* (an account of his later adventures as owner of the Rockingham track in New England). But he was the game's most innovative person during the fifties, feared and hated—a helluva combination—by at least half the people he maintained he was in partnership with. There were severe penalties for mentioning his name in jocular fashion around the office of the subservient baseball commissioner.

Veeck was pushing sixty and in a reflective mood when he submitted to an interview between jobs. He had packed in horse-racing and went back for a final shot at baseball. He was quoted as saying:

"Of all the things I've done in baseball, or anywhere else, the thing I'll be remembered most for is having sent a midget up to hit." He said it with just a tinge of bitterness.

Veeck wasn't quite accurate. He didn't send the midget up to hit, but to stand there and take four balls. You don't ask a 3'6" batter to swing away. Eddie Gaedel, the midget who was also a vaudeville performer, later recalled that Veeck, under the stands before the second game of the double-header started, had promised to brain him with a bat if he so much as swung at a pitch.

Midgets, crazy prizes aside, Veeck isn't ever going to be in any Hall of Fame, although aging fans and writers might recall him with a chuckle. There'll be no plaque with his name engraved on it. A more fitting treatment would be a tombstone with "I told them, but they wouldn't listen."

Lou Perini was a big New England construction man who had bought the Braves after World War II with a couple of his steam-shovel associates. He got lucky with pitching ("Spahn and Sain, and pray for rain") and made it into the 1948 World Series. After that it was all downhill.

For Boston the Braves' success had been a momentary diversion. It was essentially a Red Sox town, always would be. By the spring of 1953 Perini was ready to make his move to Milwaukee.

Everyone knew the Braves were gone but Perini refused to

admit it. Not only that, but he lied, no big deal in baseball where feeding twisted facts to the press was part of the agenda when the National League's first meeting was held at the Broadway Central Hotel in New York City in 1876.

He came over to Vero Beach where the Braves were playing an exhibition game with the Dodgers and with him came the newspapermen covering the Braves. It was an odd sight. The newsmen from Boston who refused to believe that there would be only one team in Boston wore one type of cap with a *B* on it. The Milwaukees wore others with *M*. "We're the Boston Braves," said the writers from Beantown. "The other thing, the *M*, stands for maybe."

It was no maybe, but just a final bit of wishful thinking. Perini was the center of a press conference while he was trying to down a hot dog. "Mr. Perini," he was asked, "do you have any plans for moving the Braves this year?" Choking slightly Perini lied, "No," in his best New England accent. The move was announced ten days later.

There was only one major change in ownership of a team between the start of the fifties and the completion. That change was in St. Louis.

Fred Saigh had bought the Cardinals from the Sam Breadon estate. He was associated with Bob Hannegan, an FDR politician. One of the hats Hannegan had worn was that of Postmaster General. It was generally agreed that Hannegan had cleared some of the obstacles out of the way for Saigh's move.

The St. Louis purchase for two and a half million or thereabouts was heralded as a steal in St. Louis and elsewhere. Insiders insisted that there was a million bucks in cold cash in the till Breadon kept just so he wouldn't run out of pocket money which was part of the deal. It was in the corporation's name, so it went along with the ball players, the uniforms and the team bus at spring training.

Saigh and Hannegan had gotten the whole thing with a loan and a small investment of their own money. Hannegan's end never came out, or if it did it was glossed over by friendly critics, but they jumped on Saigh for having gotten in with an investment of $180,000 of his own money. Not bad, putting up $180,000 to grab off a million just lying there.

Saigh was highly sensitive to criticism. "Sure," he retorted, "but I signed a note for a couple of million at the Boatman's National Bank in St. Louis, too. How many of those knocking me could walk in there and do that?"

Saigh moved swiftly into a position of inner-circle power. He teamed with the Yankees' Del Webb to lead the palace revolt which knocked Happy Chandler out of his commissioner's role. He cultivated newsmen in other cities both as sources and as conduits for news leaks. When Hannegan died unexpectedly, Saigh paid off his widow and now had the club to himself.

In 1952 under Eddie Stanky the Cardinals came close to winning the pennant. It looked like a long and successful reign for Saigh.

Then the roof caved. He was indicted for income tax evasion. He could have claimed incompetent bookkeeping but his lawyers advised him to plead nolo contendere (no defense), take the suspended sentence, pay the money and go on his way like everyone else. The judge had agreed.

When the time came for sentencing, however, there was a different judge on the bench, one who had that Judge-Roy-Bean-West-of-the-Pecos look. No defense, eh? Twenty months in the Federal pen.

It was popular gossip around baseball that all this was in retribution for the manner in which Saigh had handled Hannegan's widow in the financial arrangements. Someone had gotten to someone in Washington. A gun-slinger had been sent in at the appropriate time.

Saigh was the first owner within memory to serve time though goodness knows some warranted this treatment far more than he, including one or two who had plastered some luckless pedestrian all over the scenery while drunk driving. Saigh served five months at Evansville, Indiana, acting as a prison librarian. When he came out he was done with baseball.

Before going to prison he had sold the Cards to the Anheuser-Busch brewing people, a popular move in St. Louis. Gussie Busch, stentorian boss of the brewery, has since been a vocal and visible owner. Taking over, Busch tried to change the name of old Sportsman's Park to Budweiser (like in beer) Stadium, but the other owners balked. So it was changed to Busch Stadium, and the name was carried over to the new park down by the river, present home of the football and baseball Cardinals. Gussie got some advertising out of the name change when he came out with a Busch Bavarian brand of the foamy. But he's put a lot more into baseball than he's taken out and I've never said hello to the man.

Saigh was one of three National League owners at the start of the fifties whose main interest was baseball. Others were Horace Stoneham of the New York Giants, who had inherited the club from his father, and Bob Carpenter, a Dupont who owned the Phillies after having rescued them from bankruptcy shortly after World War II. In Brooklyn, at the start of the decade the Dodgers were owned in four equal pieces by Walter O'Malley; John Smith, the president of Charles Pfizer, which had a monopoly on the manufacture of penicillin; Branch Rickey the front-office genius who had been given a quarter share for coming in after Larry McPhail had gone off to war, and Jim Mulvey, husband of Dearie McKeever, whose father had built Ebbets Field along with Charley Ebbets.

That's a lot of name-juggling, and probably recognizable only to some of the older inhabitants who still haven't fled Brooklyn. But it's significant because ten years later, when the Dodgers beat the White Sox in the World Series, O'Malley had assumed control of the club, except for the Mulveys' 25 percent. He had bought out the John Smith share from Smith's widow and Rickey left in 1950.

Not only had O'Malley assumed control but, with his own funds, he had built Dodger Stadium in Los Angeles' Chavez Ravine. It was within view of downtown City Hall and was to be the last ball park to be built with private funds. Mountains had to be moved, literally, and O'Malley did it with the help of dozens of earth-movers. At the end of the decade O'Malley, Stoneham, and Carpenter were the three National League owners who depended, in varying degrees, on their ball clubs for a living. It was also three years since Walter Francis O'Malley, horticulturist, specialist in admiralty law, big-game hunter, president of his junior *and* senior classes at the University of Pennsylvania, master poker player and baseball manipulator, had been gone from Brooklyn. His move will be debated until the final called strike in the inter-galactic World Series.

He has alternately been branded the rogue who destroyed Brooklyn and one of the game's great innovators. His son, Peter, is president of a tidy little operation that probably is worth a hundred million dollars. His daughter Terry is a member of the board and her husband is secretary of the club. Try knocking the O'Malleys in Greater Los Angeles.

And O'Malley started from virtually nothing, using borrowed bank money for his share of equity in the flagging ball club which was on the edge of bankruptcy in the late thirties and early forties. The bank had brought in Larry MacPhail from Cincinnati to pull the operation together. Then came World War II, MacPhail's departure and Rickey's arrival from St. Louis.

In the late forties, MacPhail's earlier wheeling and dealing and Rickey's signing kids, patching, and horse-trading paid off with a couple of pennants. There were two losing seven-game series with the Yankees before hysterical crowds in '47 and '49. Now the Dodgers, and O'Malley, were ready to go it without Rickey. They did, winning five pennants in the fifties.

No one has ever decided just how much Walter O'Malley knows about baseball. Maybe he doesn't know anything but the most successful auto-dealers are those who can't tell you about a thing under that hood. But they are able to hire people who can.

O'Malley certainly seems to enjoy the game, seated in a well-appointed private box high in Dodger Stadium. He barks encouragement in gravelly tones at his employees below, but rarely does he discuss their respective merits, at least with outsiders.

He would appear to leave the talent end to those who have devoted their lives to it. And they're usually people who have worked their way up through the organization.

Al Campanis, for instance, is the vice-president in charge of player personnel. He was once an infielder with Montreal, trying without much success to make the jump from Triple-A to the big leagues. Ben Wade, the organization's chief scout, was a 19–17 lifetime righthander in the majors and the most he ever won in one year was 11 games. He's there because O'Malley thinks he can do the job better than anyone else. Having worn the Dodger blue didn't hurt, either.

It's difficult to keep O'Malley on a straight course of baseball conversation. A little gossip, a sly dig, a nugget about some other club's finances, and that's about it. He's off in the world of entertainment, politics, medicine, and literature.

O'Malley has been the game's principal king-maker for most of the last quarter-century. He has even had a hand in picking two Commissioners, the retired air force general and the former legal counsel for the National League. In the mid-seventies O'Malley's attention was diverted by a series of health problems, his own and his family's. His attention was worth ten lawyers and a couple of arbitrators to the Players Association. Many feel that had he been able to focus 100 percent on the problems confronting baseball the course of the game might have been a lot different.

When the players moved in on the cash register via the reserve-clause ruling there was no O'Malley to soothe ruffled feathers. The players' agents and lawyers had free reign. Viewing the carnage from afar the best O'Malley could muster was a rumbling, "We have met the enemy and they are us," as he watched his fellow-owners prepare to pour millions usually ticketed for player development into the pockets instead of stars-turned-free-agents.

Time had put a perfect peel-back block on the brightest and toughest of the post-war owners. Although most thought of him as the same person who had led the Dodgers West to that pot of gold and the glory of an annual attendance of almost three million, he was twenty years older. O'Malley's attitude about his career was similar to that of one of the great news executives of the fifties, the United Press's Earle Johnson. When his time came to retire from his job with the wire service they offered him a consultant's role. "No," replied Johnson, who apparently was going to have plenty to keep him occupied just following his inclinations. "And besides," he said, "Every man is of maximum service to his own generation." O'Malley's role in baseball in the fifties and sixties was crucial. It is the sport's misfortune that no one of his ilk came along in the seventies.

In the American League the fifties heavyweights were Del Webb, co-owner with Dan Topping of the Yankees, and Tom Yawkey, who had developed into a kind of patron saint in Boston because of his consideration for both players and customers alike. Both incidentally were extraordinarily rich and powerful people.

Webb, moving from humble beginnings, became the biggest Army contractor in World War II and wound up in a position to buy and sell most Western U.S. senators. He also had a hand in building a lot of those gaudy gambling temples in Las Vegas.

Yawkey was a diversified multi-millionaire, heavy into Southern lumber. He was inclined to drink and eat a great deal in the fifties. Later he gave up the booze and became an outstanding advocate of the stringent life. He lasted into his seventies, and when he finished he was about half his former girth.

Yawkey was outspoken and when asked late in life who he considered the greatest player who ever wore the Red Sox livery he skipped Ted Williams and named Carl Yastrzemski. And he didn't do it because Yaz was still playing and it might help the gate.

What always helped that department during Yawkey's tenure was his insistence that the place be shined up all the time, that there be no gouging on the hot dogs and peanuts, and that everyone have a little fun. Important men in government, business, and the arts and sciences who have come out of

Harvard became baseball nuts at Fenway. When Yawkey died in mid-'76 he was mourned unashamedly by people from Harvard Square to Scollay Square downtown, from Cape Ann at the North to the tip of Cape Cod to the South.

Webb had been a lefthanded, semi-pro pitcher on the West Coast and he too liked the booze. What cured him permanently was what he termed a miracle that didn't occur at Lourdes but in a West Coast hospital bed.

It began with a bucket of contaminated water which he drank during a Sunday game. Webb was the pitcher for the visitors. It was hot and dusty so he made frequent trips to the water bucket.

"I got typhoid," related Webb, "and it was so bad that the complications hospitalized me for a whole year. I could tell the doctors never expected me to leave the place alive. I had a lot of time to think when I was in the hospital. I figured if Roosevelt could beat what he had I could do it too. I wrote my mother and said that if I ever got out I'd never take another drink of whiskey as long as I lived." He didn't.

Webb was brought together with Dan Topping, the much-married scion of the tin-fortune people, by Larry MacPhail, who used his colonelcy in the U.S. Army to meet and greet—and play golf with—a lot of people. They grabbed off the Yankees for a steal price of around three and a half million from the pressured heirs of Colonel Jake Ruppert, the New York beer king. That was not only for the famed Yankees, but for the real estate. Two years later, the night the Yankees won the final game of the '47 Series from the Dodgers, they fired MacPhail, sending him packing with another million. MacPhail never re-entered baseball.

Through their entire tenure Webb and Topping were smart enough to stay out of the way of balls and strikes, letting Casey Stengel handle things on the field while the brooding George Weiss watched the front office. We know all about Casey's strengths; his phenomenal memory, his marvelous recuperative powers after an awesome night, his willingness to exchange even the most trivial of ideas and information with the most inconsequential of people.

Weiss's Bismarckian mind was of a different mold. Everything had to be in Prussian order at all times. Additionally he had an amazing array of super-scouts who swore fealty to him like a bunch of medieval knights. At one and the same time he had people like Paul Krichell, Tom Greenwade, Bill Essick, Gordon Jones, Bill Skiff and Joe Devine. Not only did they comb the bushes for the Mantles, McDougalds, Colemans, Richardsons, Kubeks, etc., but they stayed up with him and drank themselves owl-eyed. Few men have been accorded greater celestial benefits.

As for the Von Moltke mentality, Weiss once bawled out the Yankee Stadium's chief electrician because he didn't have two recordings of "The Star-Spangled Banner" on hand next to the public address system. The electrician stared at him in disbelief. He had just been up one of the light poles replacing a five-thousand-watter (It was the only one defunct; in some other organization it would have been ignored until a couple of additional bulbs went). Also his hernia was hurting.

"What the fuck do we want with two 'Star-Spangled Banners'?" he shouted at his Buddha-like boss. The electrician belonged to a strong union. Besides, he was the best Yankee Stadium ever had. He was entitled to one outburst a season.

"Supposing one breaks five minutes before the game?" Sheer malevolence crinkled the electrician's face. He whipped out a pocket comb.

"Here," he said, "I'll play it on this."

Just as there was money and efficiency on the Yankee team so there was miserliness and nepotism in several of the American League clubs in the fifties. In Chicago Charles Comiskey's descendents were running that franchise right into the ground.

Dorothy Comiskey was the boss of the club. (When she married Johnny Rigney, a White Sox pitcher, Rigney suddenly found himself running the club where he had once labored on the mound, just like Horatio Alger.) Young Chuck Comiskey

(Charles II) was around too, mostly in a vice-president's role. One day when the Yankees showed up at Comiskey Park the handsome young man was sporting a black eye. He said he had gotten it during a fight with a customer in the stands and the shell-shocked local Chicago writers backed up the statement.

In Washington the entire Griffith family was living off the lowly Senators. They had a big coke-making machine under the stands where they mixed the stuff with ground ice. The worse things got in the bookkeeping department the more ice they put into the drinks.

The place was loaded with nieces and nephews. Joe Haynes married Thelma Griffith and moved into the general manager's office. He too had been a pitcher with the club.

In Philadelphia the original franchise was dying painfully. Connie Mack had managed until 1950, when he was an incredible 86 (He lived to be 94). He had directed the then Athletics to a couple of World Series championships twenty years earlier when they had such luminaries as Lefty Grove, George Earnshaw, Jimmie Foxx, Al Simmons, and Mickey Cochrane. At the end he had nothing going for him except his high, starched collar and his rolled-up program which he held as he sat in the dugout.

There was no one around to pick up the fallen, sputtering torch. Mack's two sons with the club, Earle and Roy, were objects of frank derision by the press people who followed the club. Said the late Jimmy Isaminger of the *Philadelphia Inquirer:* "Connie Mack's sons became senile before Connie did." Roy did things in the front office like throwing away mail addressed to the club's promotion director. Earle was a laughing stock on the coaching lines where he wore sliding pads to give shape to his skinny haunches.

So a sale of the A's was arranged, largely engineered by Del Webb, whose construction company had rebuilt Kansas City's minor league ball park to major league capacity. He rounded up some moneyed friends in Chicago and they installed Arnold Johnson, a concessions executive, as the operating head. He didn't know too much about baseball but it turned out he didn't have to. The Yankees told him everything he had to know. "Just make sure you answer the phone when we call," they said.

The Yankees manipulated Kansas City shamelessly, as though it was still a farm club in the American Association. Writers joked about the bus that ran back and forth between New York and the then-furthest outpost in the American League. Enos Slaughter went back and forth a few times and there was a dandy cover-up on Clete Boyer, the third baseman, without a peep out of the American League or the commissioner's office.

Kansas City couldn't, and wouldn't, kick about anything the Yankees did. At various times it was estimated one-third of their entire home attendance could be traced to the Yankees' and Mickey Mantle's visits.

A dynasty departed Detroit in the fifties. The Briggs automotive family owned the club and Walter O. Briggs, the patriarch, later confined to a wheelchair behind home plate, kept the ball park as meticulous as his own front lawn. He had the biggest, fastest, and best-paid ground crew in the game. Nor did people like Al Kaline or Harvey Kuenn have to shout too much at contract time. Later Spike Briggs, a son, took over and when he became ill and died the club was sold.

2

The Lord High Executioner, Occasionally

LIKE MOST PEOPLE I was not only considerably younger twenty-five years ago but I was a good deal more innocent. People told me things and I believed them. The night Happy Chandler was fired as baseball commissioner during the meetings in St. Petersburg, Fla., a veteran newspaperman who had moved up to a position of some importance as a club executive advised, "This is a very important time in the history of our country—the changing of baseball commissioners. After all, it's the No. 2 job in the United States."

As a youth I had read this man's baseball stories in the paper, admired them, and wondered how one person could have all that information? So I believed him. I guess I carried that innocence a long way because even later, when I was fuming one day in the Yankee Stadium press box about their spending billions trying to put a man on the moon, but not being able to get me through the traffic jam on the George Washington Bridge, another sage eyed me and said softly, "You know why we're spending all that money getting a man to the moon, don't you?"

"No," I responded.

"Because," offered this oracle in sports shirt and slacks, "the first to get a man to the moon will control the earth."

"Oh, in that case," I said respectfully, "they can spend all that money and I'll take my chances with the traffic on the bridge. I don't mind being an hour and a half late for the ball game once in a while."

Today it's a different ball game, of course. If anyone ever gave me that "No. 2 job" bit now, I'd ask, "Why?" And after that I'd ask, "What's the No. 1 job in the country?"

Being baseball commissioner a quarter-century ago did, however, call for a great deal of respect, at least from the public. Baseball held an unchallenged role as the No. 1 game in the country (There go those numbers again.) and the commissioner could get his picture into the papers just about as often as he wished. He could pick his own office (that was until the TV industry and its money centered in New York) and he could be absent from his office at a ball game without suffering a guilty pang.

There have been five baseball commissioners, four of them in office during my working life. The first, Kenesaw Mountain Landis (He was named after the Civil War battle site where his father, a Union surgeon, lost a leg.) was a Midwest jurist who was brought in to "save the game." The game needed saving after the World Series fix in 1919.

Landis was a Chicago federal judge who made sure that the eight Chicago White Sox players, known later as the Black Sox, never played again even though they were found not guilty in a jury trial. Following the trial the presiding judge attended a banquet in honor of the defendants. Try keeping eight players found not guilty of charges preferred against them out of the game today and you'd probably have a hundred different court cases on charges ranging from denying a man a right to make a living to second-degree halitosis.

The iron-fisted Landis died during World War II and the

owners decided they needed a different kind of commissioner. The federal government was bigger and stronger than in the twenties when they went for Landis. How about someone with a little clout in Washington? And how about someone who wasn't able to hang up on them when they phoned because they were aware that he was carrying his signed resignation around in his breast pocket at all times?

So they tapped Albert Benjamin (Happy) Chandler, U.S. Senator from Kentucky, a good athlete in his day at Transylvania College and a fine harmonizing tenor. The owners bounced him in 1950 after he had embarrassed them by being stiff-necked when he was supposed to be compliant, and also because the players were beginning to say, "We finally got a *real* commissioner," meaning Happy had sided with them several times against the people who were paying his salary.

It took a little maneuvering to get rid of Happy, and they did it not with a vote to fire him but a vote to extend his contract. When Chandler couldn't muster enough votes for the contract-extension there was only one way for him to go—out the door.

Happy then held the job for seven or eight months. After that an intensive search for a successor was undertaken, although in retrospect it was fairly obvious that they were sitting on Happy's successor all the time. Someone leaked a story that fifty-five people had been either interviewed or had applied, including someone named Albert Chandler, whose chief qualification seems to have been that he had the same name as the man fired. Then around World Series time in 1951 they named Ford Frick who had been available all the time as president of the National League.

Among Chandler's detractors there was a story that he had buckled under the pressure of a couple first-rate damages suits by second-rate players like Danny Gardella who had jumped to the Mexican League and had been prevented from returning. Chandler, they said, trembled and ducked under the covers as the high-priced legal talent took over. This is an unlikely story since Happy knew all about threats from Southern politics. And the U.S. Senate wasn't exactly a kindergarten. It probably all went back to the time Happy momentarily forgot who was signing the checks.

Although Chandler retired to the Blue Grass country his influence was still felt in the baseball world long after his stint as commissioner. In 1952, Ford Frick's first year, there was some head-butting between the owners and the player-representatives at the annual meeting in Atlanta. The owners wanted people to believe that the players were restive about things like an extra water cooler in the dugout, or not enough towels in the locker room, but it was deeper than that. Collective bargaining was beginning to stir, although the day when the most powerful person in baseball was the executive director of the Players' Association was still twenty years up the road.

There was a coffee break and Carl Erskine, then the Brooklyn player representative, was designated to make a phone call for guidance. The man he called was Happy Chandler. Chandler gave Erskine a few pointers and back in they went to talk with their bosses and their new commissioner, Ford Frick.

Frick was the only baseball commissioner with a media background. Before he moved into the administrative end, first as a publicity man and later as National League president, he had been a reporter and radio man in New York. He was Babe Ruth's ghost-writer and this led to accusations of partisanship a couple of decades later when Roger Maris broke Ruth's sixty-homer mark for a season and Frick decreed that Roger's record in the book be accompanied by an asterisk (*).

"For crying out loud," demanded Roger, "what's this about 162 games, not 154? I did it inside 154 games, didn't I?" The record shows that Maris didn't hit his first homer until game No. 11, so he did it actually within 152 games. The asterisk is gone from the record book now but there are still two classifications, 154 game season and 162 game season. Frick was an accomplished speaker, but he didn't bother much with the media. It's rare that you get fired for something you didn't say.

A handful of owners ran baseball during Frick's regime, men

like Walter O'Malley, John Galbreath, Tom Yawkey, and Del Webb, when he could take time from rebuilding the Southwest. The game didn't need a strong figure at the top, because the challenge from football wasn't to come until the sixties. There was all kinds of movement, Braves to Milwaukee, Browns to Baltimore, Giants to San Francisco and Dodgers to Los Angeles. These matters were usually worked out on the phone between the power-brokers who later consulted with the commissioner's office.

When Walter O'Malley decided to move the Dodgers to the West Coast, taking a slightly dazed Horace Stoneham and his Giants with him ("gotta have two clubs on the coast to make the schedule workable") thereby cancelling out New York, birthplace of the National League, as a National League city, Frick was asked to step in. But he shook his head firmly and declared, "It's a league matter." His nonchalance was matched by that of the then-National League president, Warren Giles, who said, "Since when is it necessary to have New York in a league?" That was 1957; five years later the Mets were playing in the Polo Grounds.

When Frick finished in the sixties the owners felt they needed a different type of fronting executive. Military man, maybe? Good at organizing?

William D. Eckert, an Air Force general with considerable experience in accountability of material, quality control, etc., was suggested. O'Malley, again a member of the board of selectors, says he doesn't recall who suggested Eckert but that he was picked under extraordinary circumstances. The jurors were returning to New York from a final selection meeting somewhere in a private plane. They had pretty much decided on Eckert, overlooking his obvious inability to communicate with the media and presumably the fans. Just before the plane was scheduled to land the pilot called back into the cabin, "Hey, I think something funny has happened to New York. It's all dark."

It was that first record blackout. The plane turned around and went to Philadelphia. No one considered this to be an omen.

They stuck with the general for a few years and his steward-ship generated a couple of entertaining newspaper stories. When the announcement was made they had appointed Gen. William Eckert as commissioner, Larry Fox, a New York newsman, could be pardoned for blurting a slightly stunned "Who?" The baseball spokesman repeated the name in full. "Jeez," said Larry, "They went and got the Unknown Soldier."

Some time into the general's tenure his publicity man thought it might be nice if he got a little friendly with the newspaper writers who covered the game on a daily basis. Best place would be their annual meeting. Having Eckert available would be no problem because the Baseball Writers Association's annual meeting is always held concurrent with the annual baseball meetings.

Eckert arrived, shook a few hands, fumbled around for a bunch of index cards with a rubber band around them, placed them on the podium, and started his talk, turning the cards slowly.

The writers looked at each other. Cards? And what was this about production goals, work incentives, etc.

"Hey," stage-whispered someone quicker than the rest, "He got his cards mixed up. This is supposed to be the speech for the engineers at Lockheed!" Eckert hastily stowed the cards in his pocket, stumbled through a short speech and left.

3

The Old Man

IF FORD FRICK let it ring when newspaper people phoned, the same could scarcely be said of Casey Stengel, the top baseball personality of the fifties. You wanted Stengel? Hold the phone, be right there. A face-to-face, one-on-one discussion? Meet me downstairs in the bar in ten minutes. Sure, I remember ya. Didn't I meetcha at the meetings in L. A. ten years ago?

Casey had his date with the One Big Scorer in Sept. 1975. There were so many at his funeral they overflowed the chapel at Forest Lawn. People came from everywhere to pay solemn-visaged tribute. They stayed to exchange Stengel stories. Check the last time there was suppressed laughter at a funeral for a celebrity. Stengel stories were always a cut above others.

He certainly generated enough of them in his more than half-century in baseball. And in the fifties he was at his peak as a winner and as a leader.

Casey Stengel actually grew better-looking as he got older.

Not that he was any beauty contest winner but those pictures of him as a player for Uncle Robbie in Brooklyn or John McGraw in the Polo Grounds showed a sort of wise-ass with big ears, heavy legs, and a knowing smile. In his sixties, the years which carried him through the decade of the fifties, his face had assumed a seamy dignity. He wore his hair in an old-fashioned part, plastered flat. The eyes still danced.

Stengel was a rich man able to do the thing he most wanted to twenty-four hours a day. To use one of his choicer phrases, you'd hafta say he was one in a milyun.

Stengel's interest in baseball was all encompassing and he vacuumed bits of information from everywhere. His end objective always was to win; if he didn't he figured he had done something incorrectly. Retracing his steps you'd usually find that key spot and usually you'd find it wasn't Casey's error.

Take the grounder that skidded off a pebble and hit Tony Kubek, the Yankee shortstop, in the throat, giving the Pirates the 1960 World Series over the Yankees. Casey was accustomed to getting by on very little sleep (He had it down to about four hours by the fifties) but even had he stayed up all night concentrating he wouldn't have been able to come up with an answer to a pebble being in the wrong place in Forbes Field.

He won a lot of World Series, starting in 1949, when the Yankees brought him in as a sort of well-seasoned clown who was supposed to win where Bucky Harris had lost to the Indians and Red Sox the year before. He ran off five in a row and that record for winning World Series is going to stand a while.

Casey had help, of course, in the tremendous flow of talent directed to the Yankees by their scouts, along with their incredibly sharp front-office people, but when it came down to the "play ball" phase it was Casey's to win or lose.

I think of Casey a good deal these days, quote him a lot. When Billy Martin, a special Stengel protege, lost the 1976 World Series in four straight to the Cincinnati Reds, he ran and hid from the press. I thought of how Stengel would have reacted. Tough as Martin is, and with the forty-year spread in their ages,

Casey probably would have grabbed him, spun him around, and ordered, "Get out there and talk to them reporters, dammit. You're the manager of the Yankees!"

I think of Stengel when the agent of some .280 hitter negotiates a three-year contract for a million (Stengel was a .280 hitter himself) and wonder what he would think about all that money. Stengel was never concerned about how much people did or didn't make. What would have bothered him would have been the flow of all that money out of the game.

When Stengel played he made comparatively good money for his day, maybe five thousand, seven thousand, or eight thousand dollars a year. His wife Edna did well in California real estate. He saved his money and when the time came where do you think he invested some of it? In baseball. He bought a piece of the Worcester Club in the old Class A Eastern league. The local people whom he had bailed out were so surprised and thankful they made him general manager and president.

The club did only passably well and the time came for a managerial change. So President Stengel fired Manager Stengel, protecting his investment. If you stretch both hands before you and count all the fingers you see that's probably two or three more than the total number of major league players who have put their money back into baseball. Count Stengel as one.

I think of Stengel sometimes when I think of my father, dead forty years. He went early, a troubled man, and I never knew what bothered him. He was a skilled mechanic who held a good job during the Great Depression and he stuck around long enough to see my first by-line in a big-league paper. But there was never much communication between us, even on the day I took him to the hospital and both he and I knew he was never coming out of the place.

I think I am a fairly strong-fibered, self-reliant newsman, and I never had to go to anyone with a big problem. But if I ever had, Stengel would have been my man. I listened to him the way I would have liked to have listened to my father.

Case in point: By mid-summer a newspaperman on the baseball beat has seen at least a hundred games, counting spring training, and there's another hundred coming up, so he tends to become a little fuzzy in the press box. Heywood Hale Broun, himself a baseball writer before becoming an actor and then a TV personality, likened a newsman's role to playing in a successful Broadway play which was in the middle of a long run. "The lines tend to get a little blurry," said Broun. "It gets tough to concentrate."

It's also easy to get involved in attention-diverting conversation or in scanning the stands for friends and good-looking women. When you do you must inevitably miss things.

One day during a hilarious exchange with *The New York Time*'s Lou Effrat, I missed a play. It wasn't catastrophic, since I got no further with my mistake than the post-game discussion in the manager's office but as soon as I delivered an opinion I could tell from the looks I had blown it. Stengel just looked at me, said nothing.

After the crowd started to disperse he gave me the you-stay-here finger wave, and said, "Lissen, if you watch the ball you'll always know what's going on. That's all ya gotta remember. If it's in the pitcher's hand, watch it. When he throws it, watch it. If the batter swings and misses, watch the ball. Or if he hits it, watch it, and don't worry about what's going on on the bases. That way you'll always know what's happening."

I know Stengel's advice stayed with me because last summer I found myself repeating it, almost verbatim, to a young newsman.

Stengel's ethical sense probably was stronger than most. When co-owner Del Webb took his championship Yankees to train in Phoenix in 1951 he attempted to do all sorts of nice things for the fellas from New York. Many of the newsmen were veterans and had covered the Yankees in the glory days of the thirties and forties, before Webb and Topping owned the club. For instance, the Yankee broadcaster, Mel Allen, was a hundred-fold better known than any of his employers.

To accommodate these guys there were barbecues, personnel

from his construction company at anyone's beck and call, and fifty dollar Stetsons in which to pose for Western pictures. There was even a stock tip, not from Webb directly but passed along through the club's P.R. man.

Something's come up where Del thinks you can make a little money without a lot of trouble. An investment."

Then he explained that one of Webb's big-shot friends had found some crazy old miner who had stumbled onto a uranium mine and had taken it over. Uranium was very big in the early fifties. The world was going to function on atomic power, and uranium was the stuff that was going to fuel it. "So," the P.R. man said, "if you got any broker friends at home give them a ring and tell them to pick you up some Little Star Uranium on the over-the-counter."

The newsmen forgot all about the local phenoms performing that day—kids like Mickey Mantle, Gil McDougald, Tom Morgan, all graduates of a previous instructional school Casey had run earlier in the month in Phoenix. They ran for the phones. All except me.

I ran for Casey. Yes, Casey had heard about what was going on. Yes, he thought it might be a good buy and a chance to make a little money. Was Casey going to get some, too?

Stengel stopped short, looked at me. "You askin' me whether I'm recommending something to you I wouldn't buy myself?"

"No," I stammered, "I just wanted to know whether you liked it?"

"Of course I like it and you can bet I'm getting some of it. Do you think I'd tell you to get it without getting it myself? Anyone who would do that doesn't . . . " and Casey fought for a simile, "doesn't belong on this earth. They should push him right off." That was Stengel's estimate of anyone who would shill for something inferior and try to stick friends with it.

There's a sequel to the Little Star Uranium story. What looked like a lot of uranium ore turned out to be a relatively small deposit. Not enough for big profits or even little ones. After it had sagged to almost zero on the daily quotes it was absorbed by something called Anshutz Drilling. I think the certificates are still around, somewhere. I wonder whether they found Casey's in the wild melange of stuff he left behind when he died in 1975.

Casey never felt quite comfortable with TV. Radio people were okay but the newspapers and newspapermen were his main sources of information. He respected them, worked with them, favored them shamelessly. He was a newspaper nut, buying every paper available as soon as he hit a new town. Then he'd fold them under his arm and sit in the hotel lobby and discourse. Later you'd see him at the park and you wondered how he had time to absorb everything that was in the papers because he certainly knew what was going on. And not only in baseball. Some of us thought he read them in the elevator going up to his room to get his stuff to go out to the park.

He wasn't too comfortable with magazine people although he nicked the old *Saturday Evening Post* for more than a hundred thousand dollars for his life story after the Yankees fired him. The life story turned out to be a little short of a full life; Stengel was to have a reincarnation as manager of the New York Mets, preaching of the marvelous opportunities available in baseball to the "youth of the nation," particularly with the New York Mets who were to lose 231 games in their first two seasons.

In the mid-fifties *Life* magazine was probably the biggest thing in the business. A press agent planting a cover story therein could figure on living off his feat for the next five years. They decided to do a story on Casey and dispatched one of their better men to try to etch him in living prose. The writer caught up with the club in Boston at the Hotel Kenmore during a difficult period for the Yankees. The pitching suddenly seemed to have gone to Hell; Mantle and the big hitters were sitting around looking at their manicures. Stengel sought to throw a little light on the future in the dimly lit Kenmore bar.

The corner in which the writer spotted him was a little brighter than the rest of the place, thanks to Stengel. He was wearing a pair of orange slacks which his wife had been imploring him to donate to the next clothing drive. He loved those slacks, however, or rather he loved the fellow who had given them to him as a present. Dammit, he'd wear what he pleased. He wasn't hurting anyone, was he?

Also he was into the scotch at this particular moment. Casey was an unusual drinker. If someone pours down ten or twelve scotches he can be assumed to qualify as a heavy drinker. Heavy drinkers usually take it with a splash of water. Stengel demanded soda in every one. The carbonation from a dozen drinks has to make you feel like the Goodyear blimp.

But he drank them that way, right to the end, the pinkie stuck out like the society ladies. That's the way the *Life* writer discovered him—visible, vocal and available.

He came away with the impression of a gravel-voiced drunk, and unfortunately wrote the story that way. Matter of fact his lead paragraph spoke of a baggy-pants clown arguing in a saloon after winning a game or losing a game, and how could anyone run a ball club the following day? He obviously knew nothing of Stengel's extraterrestrial recuperative powers which enabled him to bounce up after two or three hours of sleep and go sailing off to the park ahead of everyone else except perhaps the trainer and the equipment man.

When Stengel saw the story he exploded. He demanded to know what right they had to write about him that way (none), and whether they were willing to let others examine the life styles and habits of their writers (no). "Let him come around the ball park at 9:30 in the morning, if he's up," he stormed. "I'll be there working."

There wouldn't be much point reconstructing Casey's quarter-century-old pique over a magazine piece in a publication no longer around in its old form, except for an interesting epilogue.

Casey won the pennant that year and again in 1957 and 1958. In 1959 he finished third behind Al Lopez's White Sox and Joe Gordon's Indians. He found himself in the somewhat novel situation of having nothing to do after the season except go home to Glendale and worry about the neighborhood kids possibly drowning each other in his pool. In all the years I knew Casey,

incidentally, I never saw him in a pair of swimming trunks and
no one knew whether he even could swim. He might have been a
little sensitive about the weird-looking bone formation on his leg,
the result of an auto accident when he was managing Boston, of
which you'll hear more later.

But he didn't go back to Glendale. He went to the World
Series, held in Comiskey Park, Chicago, and the Coliseum in Los
Angeles, the Dodgers' temporary home where it drew three
straight crowds of ninety thousand, which will probably remain
an all-time record. There he was, behind the batting cage
admiring Ted Kluszewski's batting practice swings just like the
341 other media people busy interviewing each other. (Klu
singled and homered off Roger Craig that day, and homered
again off Sandy Koufax, so it paid to pay attention.)

The big item, however, was Casey's press tag. "*Life* Magazine"
was how it read. Casey Stengel working for *Life?* Weren't those
the guys who had called him a drunk, a clown, etc?

"What about it?" snapped Stengel, "plenty of people have
called me worse. And they're right here, around this here
batting cage." He paused. "And anyway, I can't hold a hate."

So he puttered his literary way through the series, put in a
final year with the Yankees in which he lost on that pebble-
bounce to the Pirates, and was fired. He was out of the game in
1961 while the Mets tooled up. In his capacity of vice-president
of the Valley National Bank in Glendale, Stengel presumably
told funny baseball stories to those who were turned down on
business loans.

He never said an unkind word about the Yankee people who
had employed him and then let him go along with his friend
George Weiss, the general manager, who in turn became Mets
president and hired Casey in 1962. When the Yankees announced he was going, Casey said, "I've been paid in full. It's a
question of whether a man should work after a certain time. I
was told my services would not be desired any longer with this
ball club. I had not much of an argument."

He was seventy, and if the people who paid the bills felt that age to be too old, how could he hold a hate against them?

He couldn't even hold a hate against people who would have laughed if they stumbled over him lying in the gutter. With the Mets, Howard Cosell went after his job. Stengel never mentioned his name.

Earlier there was a Boston columnist, Dave Egan. Harvard-trained, he threw in a bit of extra vitriol daily, hopeful that it would sell additional copies of the since-gone tabloid for which he wrote. Sometimes he outdid himself as in Stengel's final unhappy season as manager of the Braves. One rainy night he was trying to cross a street and was run down. His leg was broken badly, forcing him to walk with that rolling gimp for the remainder of his life. The driver, of course, was uninsured.

Egan waited for the end of the year, traditionally the time when awards are made in sports. Then with a strong disregard for facts, he wrote that the prize for having done the most for Boston baseball that year should go to the cab driver (actually it was a private car) which had hit Stengel. The line got wide circulation and all of Boston chuckled. Some of Egan's colleagues said, enviously, "Boy, the colonel really got Casey with that one."

Stengel out-lived Egan but that unsightly knob on his leg just above the ankle was a constant reminder of "the person who had done the most for Boston baseball."

Baseball had taken its furthermost step West in 1955 by switching the Athletics' franchise from Philadelphia to Kansas City. Del Webb had found some Chicago money which would buy out the Connie Mack family, guarantee a job or two, and the league moved the franchise into the Kansas City ball park. Webb's interest was that his company had the contract to rebuild the park there to major-league proportions.

In that first year the new K.C. Athletics drew a million, with more than a third coming from the eleven home games played with the Yankees. (The A's miraculously won four of them.)

The Yankees stayed at the Muehlebach Hotel downtown, a hostelry famous for having once been the poker-playing home-away-from-home for Harry S. Truman. After a night game the Yankees returned and on his way into the all-night coffee shop Stengel bought a copy of the next morning's paper. A newspaperman accompanying him also decided to invest a dime.

"Hey, lookit this," he exclaimed over a dish of bacon and eggs, "Dave Egan died." And he looked to Stengel for his reaction.

Stengel picked his words carefully. "The man drank," he said. "When his bosses wanted to fire him, I saved his job. Now he's dead."

Now Stengel's dead too and no one will ever know whether he saved Dave Egan's job before or after Egan wrote that line about the driver who hit Stengel.

It's safe to say that for most of the time Stengel was with the Yankees there was at least one player who earned a bigger salary than he. He inherited DiMaggio, a one-hundred-thousand-dollar performer, and after a while there were men like Mantle, Berra, and Ford pushing up to that level. Ford and Mantle also had an arrangement which even Stengel couldn't qualify for—on the road they signed at the hotel for anything they wanted. The bill just went to the Yankees. This was a move made in gratitude for this pair's never having given the club a hard time on contract negotiations.

Stengel stayed clear of money talk with his players at all times. The "office" handled such matters. George Weiss, his No. 2 man, Roy Hamey, and sundry assistants, dealt with the players and they seemed to do well with everyone except Yogi Berra.

Yogi was a three-times winner of Most Valuable Player honors and all he got was a trophy. He wanted it translated into cash, especially after the third time when he realized he had won as many as he was going to. In his money talks he was getting nowhere with Weiss, the empire builder, and blurted out that sentiment. "Lemme talk to your bosses," ordered Yogi. It was one of the few times Dan Topping or Del Webb got into the money picture.

Bismarckian and austere in a pudgy sort of way, George Weiss enjoyed a career which virtually paralleled Stengel's even down to gaining membership in the Hall of Fame only a few years after Stengel did. They went back almost a half century to when Weiss owned a club in the Eastern League and one of his rivals was the Worcester club which had Stengel wearing those three hats. The garrulous ex-major leaguer and the taciturn son of a New Haven grocer who had never gone further than managing his high school team, found and cleaved to each other through various vicissitudes, rescuing each other, time and again. When Weiss had to fire the highly popular Bucky Harris after the Yankees' collapse in 1948, his ace was Casey Stengel out in Oakland, managing in the Pacific Coast League.

Stengel made it as a major-league manager in Brooklyn in the early thirties but Weiss didn't come up to the majors until 1947. He had been operating the Yankee farm system from a sort of control center with the Newark Bears in the International League. Ed Barrow, who ran the Yankees for years and had all kinds of World Series victories to show for it in the thirties and forties, wisely decided that Weiss's most effective spot was with *talent*, a notch below the majors.

Then Webb, Topping and Larry MacPhail entered the picture and Barrow was gone. With MacPhail there could be only one No. 1, himself. Weiss's light had a few extra bushels heaped on it, but he never let up sending the talent onward and upward. The Berras, Rizzutos, Bobby Browns, Jerry Colemans, and the rest kept coming through the pipeline to Yankee Stadium.

Weiss was both smart and lucky. He was surrounded by associates who were also friends, people like Billy Meyer, Johnny Neun, Bill Skiff, Paul Krichell, all of whom could get through that forbidding facade he offered. They all also had that amazing sixth sense for talent. Weiss's creed was a kind of reverse of the "never trust anyone over thirty" philosophy prevalent among the young in the sixties. "Never trust anyone you didn't work with in the minors," was the way he figured.

He signed Rizzuto personally, ringing the family's doorbell out in the Queens section of New York after the Giants had advised Rizzuto, "Why'n't you go get yourself a shoebox, kid?" It was an act of faith that had to be good for a couple of American League pennants. When the Yankees brought Berra up in 1946 and some of the smart ones in the press box, accustomed to graceful performers behind the plate like Bill Dickey and Aaron Robinson, said things like "How can he be a catcher? His arms are too short," or "He looks more like a bartender than a catcher," only the ghost of a smile crossed Weiss's face. It might even have been a grimace. Berra, with three MVP's (Most Valuable Player Awards) and Rizzuto with one, accounted for almost half those awards in the 1950s. Mickey Mantle, signed by Tom Greenwade for $1,150, accounted for two more. All three represented a bonus outlay of around eight thousand dollars.

Greenwade was an Ozark character with about a 190 IQ in and out of baseball. Indoors he'd chew thoughtfully on a toothpick, outdoors on a blade of grass. What a way to murder the slickers. Yet he was slick enough to represent the Internal Revenue Service around Springfield, Missouri, during part of his career.

Greenwade's arrangement with Weiss was interesting. Weiss always demanded an itinerary. He had to know where everyone was. Greenwade balked. "You want me, call my number. If I'm not there my wife will get the message to me." Every time George's gorge rose over this flouting of authority, he thought of Mickey Mantle hitting homers from either side of the plate.

The ultra-smooth operation of this superb talent machine enabled Stengel to appear like some latter-day Houdini. He needed a twenty-game winner in 1954 when his big pitchers started to slip. Up came a tough young righthander, Bob Grim, to win twenty and take rookie of the year honors. Where did they get Grim? From the farm system of course, but he was scouted on a subway ride over to Brooklyn where his folks ran a neighborhood saloon in which Bob tended bar in the off-season.

The strength of their minor league clubs enabled Weiss to make all kinds of deals for pitchers. Inevitably some were busts, like Harry Byrd, a winner with the lowly A's who flopped with the Yankees. Then there was Bob Turley, who came from Baltimore to be the Yankee's first Cy Young Award winner.

With him in a sixteen-player deal came Don Larsen, who lost more than he won in his major league career, but who pitched the only perfect game in World Series history for the Yankees against the Dodgers in 1956.

Three Yankee first-year men won rookie honors in the fifties— Gil McDougald in 1951, Grim in 1954, and Tony Kubek in 1957.

The genius of George Weiss was that he could, and did, put together all kinds of winners. Sometimes he did it with an array of power hitters, other times there'd be three pitchers, just about even in ability like Raschi, Reynolds and Lopat, and if you were still standing he'd whistle for some kid like Whitey Ford to come up with a 9-and-1 mark just for the frosting.

Take the 1951 club which went on to win the World Series in six games from the Giants after being humbled by Lefty Dave Koslo in the opener. Stengel was right in the middle of that fabulous five-Series streak and theoretically should have been at the height of his strength. Wrong.

A little quote from the *Official Baseball Guide* of that year: "The Yankees achieved their '51 championship with one .300 swatter, rookie Gil McDougald (.306) and without a single member in the 100-RBI class. . . . Another freshman who played an important role was Mickey Mantle, a shortstop at Joplin (Western Association) in 1950. Mantle was converted into an outfielder during the spring. Although he quickly mastered the tricks of this new job the twenty-year-old's hitting failed to measure up to expectations and on July 15 he was shipped to Kansas City. Mickey rejoined the Bombers on August 24 and hiked his American League mark from .260 to .267 in the remaining weeks."

They were talking about a youth who, five years later, would hit almost 100 percentage points higher, en route to the Triple Crown of average, homers, and runs batted in. The Yankees won the 1951 Series but the *Guide* couldn't find anyone on the club worthy of putting on its front cover. It went instead, with Stan Musial, who had won the National League batting crown for the fifth time, not a bad accomplishment, either.

Well, what did win for the '51 Yankees? Probably pitching—

twenty-one-game winners in Raschi and Lopat, and seventeen for Reynolds, including a league-leading seven shutouts, with two no-hitters.

Stengel's attitudes as a ball player earlier fashioned his thinking about player deportment when it was time for him to become the leader. He never indicated a .300 hitter could perhaps get it up to .325 if he observed curfew like the rest. He had broken too many rules along the way himself. A fellow who once had fought a teammate down five flights of stairs, rolling and bumping like in some bad TV movie, could be inclined to take a lenient outlook on things like an extra drink, hour, or girl.

Weiss however could never bring himself to accept the fact that there were people making more money than he had ever dreamt of at their age now flouting rules which in the end could help them make even more. The only way to handle these ingrates, if Casey wouldn't, would be through private detectives.

Shortly after the Yankees had wrapped up the 1958 pennant, Weiss got word of a burst of post-midnight activity among the top players on a western trip. They came over from Kansas City to Detroit, and there was a bit of nonsense on the train about Ryne Duren getting looped and trying to shove Ralph Houk's cigar back into his face. This was superb thinking on Duren's part; Houk, then one of Stengel's coaches, had been a Ranger captain in the U.S. infantry in World War II. He barely accorded ol' Rhino the courtesy of recognizing this overt move. Merely flipping a light backhand at him, he caught Duren over the eyebrow with his World Series ring. Duren's bottle-bottom glasses flew off, and a slight cut appeared over his eye. He promptly fell into a fit of weeping and had to be led off to bed, Houk assisting.

It got back to Weiss and he figured things better be stopped right there. He wasn't worried about Duren too much. The entertaining reports turned out to be on Ford and Mantle. He assigned a professional gumshoe to tail this tandem in Detroit.

The club got back to the Hotel Statler after a night game in

Briggs Stadium and there was this private eye—Panama hat, brown and white shoes, yellowish-tan sports jacket, the whole bit from Central Casting—standing in the lobby trying to look like a fan. He attempted to engage one or two players in conversation without much luck. Finally he approached Whitey Ford. "I'm a big fan from up on the peninsula," he offered, "but I don't get down to the games too much, and I don't recognize any of the Yankee players. Which ones are Ford and Mantle?"

Ford had been tipped off. He saw Tony Kubek and Bobby Richardson, the shortstop-second base combination and the team's original clean-livers, just going out the door for a bit of late refreshment. "Ford and Mantle?" he repeated. "There they go, right out that door."

"Thanks," said the dick hastily, and he took off after Kubek and Richardson, barely missing getting his nose caught in the revolving door.

Ford could hardly wait for breakfast. "Where'd you guys go last night?" he asked innocently. "You seemed to be in one helluva hurry."

"We were," responded Richardson, "there's a place that makes great sodas but they don't stay open past 12:30 and we wanted to make it."

Casey Stengel is the only manager I ever knew who was arrested in one of those come-along-with-us situations, but it wasn't over that earlier-mentioned fight down the five floors of stairs. The pinch came forty years later when he was an apparently respected national figure.

First, the fight, of which there are several versions. The one Casey told me springs from an explanation of why he had a deep furrow extending from the lower corner of his mouth, though my reason for asking about it is long forgotten.

"Pitcher name of Whitey Appleton give it to me in Brooklyn," he recalled. "He was from Texas and we wuz roommates. One day when we had the day off and we went out to Coney Island which was very fancy in them days and where I had met a nice family which had a couple of nice young daughters. They give a party and invited me and told me I could bring a friend so I brought Appleton. It was okay except they had a punch bowl that had something kinda strong in it and my friend got into it and after a while he started to make some remarks to the girls so I figured I'd better get him home.

"It's a long ride on that trolley in them days all the way from Coney Island back to downtown Brooklyn where we lived and he's got all that time to think about things and get mad. He starts arguing with me the minute we get into the house and start to climb them five floors of stairs. By the time we got to the top he's ready and he jumps me but I'm ready, too, and we fight our way back down all them stairs, bouncing around, mostly on our heads. He gets his fingers inside my mouth and rips me. Here."

Casey pointed to the scar which time had failed to obliterate.

"By the time we're at the bottom both of us are finished and we shook hands and climbed up the stairs to the apartment. The next day Uncle Robbie says, 'Hey, both you guys look kinda funny, and how come you're wearing your hats in the clubhouse?' He doesn't know that if we take them off he'll see all them bumps on our heads. We had so many it was tough getting our hats on."

More than sixty years later I looked up Whitey Appleton in the *Baseball Encyclopedia*. He had a lifetime won-lost record in the majors of 5 and 12.

There were no blows struck at the time of Casey's only known arrest, only an alleged kick. It was at spring training in St. Petersburg in 1956 or 1957. A photographer from the afternoon paper, the *Independent*, got in the way of Stengel's view of the field. Casey said he shouted him out of the way; the photographer claimed Stengel had kicked him out of the way. He went back and complained to his managing editor who took it to the publisher, who ordered the photographer to file an assault charge.

First thing Stengel knew about it was after dinner when a couple of St. Pete cops showed up asking for him. Stengel thought they were looking for an autograph. They had a warrant for his arrest and off they went to the station house. It didn't create much of a stir around the ancient Hotel Soreno, where the Yankees were quartered. Most of the customers thought the cops were taking Stengel down to the morgue to identify an old friend.

Then Bob Fishel, the Yankee press agent, got a call. It was Stengel at the police station. "They want fifty bucks," shouted Casey.

"Who does?" asked Fishel.

"The cops," answered Stengel.

"For what?"

"To let me go."

"What did you do?"

"Nuthin'," said the maestro.

"Be right there," advised Fishel. "Don't talk to any reporters."

Fishel turned over the bail money and drove Stengel back to the hotel. Stengel was fuming. "Jeez," he said, "arrested. At my age."

"Don't talk to any reporters," advised Fishel again.

Fifteen minutes after he was back the whole hotel knew Stengel had been pinched. And the morning paper headlined it as though it was another Sputnik in orbit.

It was both a joke and a potential disaster—Stengel being arrested. That was like running in George Washington or Nathan Hale. And for kicking a photographer, which a lot of people thought could be an excellent idea. On the other hand the publisher of the paper, a Canadian, really didn't care about American folk heroes and had ordered the now-reluctant photographer to go the limit. "Sue him for all he's got," was the word.

Cooler heads on the Chamber of Commerce stepped in. The Yankees were St. Pete's prize adornment during the winter months. Anything happens to Stengel, goodbye Yankees, also several million bucks worth of tourism.

There were a couple of hurried conferences among the Chamber people, the cops, the photographer, the publisher. Out of it came the reluctant, "We'll take an apology."

Stengel shook his grizzled head. No apology. Bob Fishel ran to the typewriter and knocked out a couple of paragraphs of an apology, Stengel-style. When Stengel was insisting there was nothing to apologize over, Fishel turned the I'm sorry document over to the local people, and the cops gave him his fifty bucks back. Fishel had Stengel saying that he didn't do it but if he did he was certainly sorry because this fellow was a war veteran and Stengel was a war veteran himself (World War I, Navy) and he'd never think of kicking a fellow war veteran.

All this happened early Saturday morning, giving the writers plenty of time to write sizable stories for the Sunday papers which provided more space than on weekdays. Stengel's malfeasance was page one up North, just as it was in Florida.

The Yankees played a game that afternoon at Al Lang field and after it was over Stengel sat around fully clad in his uniform except for his shoes. His feet were up on his desk. Most of the questioning had taken place; everyone had just about left. I turned and over my shoulder I asked, "Did you kick him, Casey?"

Casey glared. "You didn't see any blood on him, didja?"

The famous Copacabana incident also involved the law, but Casey was not in that one. Some of his better players got their names in the papers over a fight which did or didn't take place at a Yankee party. Mickey Mantle, Yogi Berra, Billy Martin, Hank Bauer, and Johnny Kucks, the pitcher, were out with their wives. Someone passed a remark and a short time later someone flattened him in the men's room. When the guy came to, he claimed he had been belted by Hank Bauer. Big headlines and shortly thereafter the club announced everyone had been fined one thousand dollars except Johnny Kucks who wasn't making that kind of money. Kucks was stuck for five hundred dollars.

The fellow who was belted turned out to be a delicatessen store owner from uptown. He sued Bauer for big money and he lost. Then the judge advised that Hank could, in turn, sue him for defamation of character, etc., but Hank said, what would happen if he won? One thing he didn't need was a delicatessen. Everyone dropped all charges.

Except George Weiss. He decided that Billy Martin was the ringleader who was getting everyone into trouble. He sent him to Kansas City in a seven-player deal, part of which was the acquisition of Ryne Duren by the Yankees. The Yankees also threw in Series pitcher Ralph Terry, and Woodie Held, an infielder-outfielder. Weiss whispered to a few intimates that if he hadn't gotten rid of Martin he'd have "destroyed the club." Billy Martin immediately insisted that it was all Casey's fault for not standing up for him, a typical son-versus-father accusation. For a couple of seasons he avoided Casey. After a while he realized how silly he was acting, and he made make-up overtures which Stengel accepted.

Out of the Copa incident came a pretty good quote from Bauer, a Marine who had picked up a load of shrapnel in his back in the Pacific. Said Hank: "If I really hit the guy the way he said I did he wouldn't have been around to sue me."

When Stengel departed in 1960, the Yankees also paid off Weiss with a five-year agreement that called for his not acting as a general manager for any other team in the majors. He didn't. He simply assumed the presidency of the New York Mets and phoned Stengel.

Building the Mets with re-treads, kids and kooks, was a slow process. Casey carried the operation virtually on his shoulders alone until 1965 when he suffered a freak hip-shattering accident getting out of a car. They gave him a stainless steel joint and the doctors said at 75 he'd probably last a year or two. And in a little while he'd be immobilized because very few of those steel joints worked with a person his age.

He fooled them completely. He went ten more and he was practically sprinting around most of the time. At the last Old Timers Day he attended at Shea Stadium the end was only a couple of months off but there he was, entering from center field in a chariot which they found goodness knows where, holding the reins on a couple of superannuated milk-wagon haulers.

Then he was gone and like he was everyone's father, everyone felt remiss in not having spent more time with him, particularly at the end. Billy Martin was out in front here. He was so distraught he went to Casey's home in Glendale after the funeral and proceeded to sleep in Casey's bed three straight nights. It was Billy's way of saying "I'm sorry."

Which would probably be the last thing Casey Stengel would have wanted anyone to say. Including himself. His philosophy was "You do the best y'can, dammit and that's it. You win some and you lose some and I've been in this game a long time and if you do good work y'don't hafta worry about a thing."

Work? One of the stories they told at his funeral was when he was managing those dreadful first-year Mets. The Cincinnati Reds had won the National League pennant the previous year and off that, Fred Hutchinson, their manager, had been named to manage the National League all-stars. One of the coaches he invited to be on the squad was his old pal Casey.

President Kennedy was in attendance in the Washington ball park and Stengel was ushered over to shake hands. They chatted pleasantly. There were other people waiting to be introduced but Kennedy was loathe to let Stengel go. Finally Stengel started shifting from one foot to the other. Then he stuck out his hand for a final shake and said, "Excuse me, Mr. President, but I hafta go to work."

4

Other Members of the Fraternity

LEST THERE BE AN ERRONEOUS IDEA that all major league clubs in the fifties were managed by Casey Stengel, it should be pointed out that there were other men—some of them extraordinarily gifted—guiding non-Yankee teams during that decade. Six are in the Hall of Fame along with Casey. They include Al Lopez, the only manager to beat Stengel in a pennant race during that decade (1954, Cleveland; 1959, Chicago), and a couple of other Yankee managers who preceded him, Joe McCarthy and Bucky Harris.

Other managers of the fifties who have been installed in the Cooperstown pantheon are Rogers Hornsby, quite possibly the finest righthanded hitter who ever lived; Lou Boudreau, who managed a couple of clubs after winning it all with the '48 Indians as a player-manager, and Connie Mack, who managed the Philadelphia Athletics for a half-century into 1950.

The fifties offered a wide choice in managers. Homespun and folksy? Try Burt Shotton, who lost the National League's 1950 pennant on the last day of the season to the Phillies. Burt was bounced not because of this but because he was a lifetime friend of Branch Rickey, ticketed to be pushed out of the Dodger presidency.

Piratical? Try Leo Durocher, a pennant winner with the Giants in 1951 and 1954 and the mastermind of an incredible sweep over the 1954 Indians in the World Series. The Indians had as good a pitching staff as ever was assembled. Early Wynn, Bob Lemon, and Bob Feller subsequently were voted into the Hall of Fame. The Giants ate 'em alive.

Scholarly? Try Eddie Sawyer, ex-professor of zoology who led the Phillies to their first flag in thirty-five years. They lost four straight—all close—to the Yankees. Later in the decade Sawyer, in his second tour of duty in Philadelphia, quit after opening day with the line "I'm forty-nine and I want to live to be fifty." Not as good as Durocher's "Nice guys finish last" but not bad for a final bow.

Schemers? Try Eddie Stanky and Solly Hemus with the Cardinals. As a Giant base-runner Stanky kicked a ball out of Phil Rizzuto's hand to break up a 1951 World Series double-play in what had to be the classic demonstration of pin-point kicking. Eddie had been a soccer player in his youth around Philadelphia. Solly Hemus could stand in there and take a fast ball in the ribs for that free trip to first base better than 90 percent of the men he played with and against. He wore a shirt three sizes too large. Loose folds counted when you were trying to fool the umpire.

Longevity? There's Walt Alston, not looking a great deal differently today from that afternoon in 1954 when he assumed charge of the Dodgers at their Vero Beach training base, picking up the torch wrested out of Charley Dressen's grasp. Jolly Cholly had taken the Dodgers to two flags after blowing the 1951 pennant to the Giants on Bobby Thomson's epic homer in the ninth inning of that final playoff game. Alston's major league record showed one at bat with the Cardinals. He was a first-base replacement and the Cubs' Lon Warnecke struck him out. Warnecke later became a National League umpire.

Dressen was fired because he let his wife urge him into demanding a three-year contract. Their fairly reasonable premise was that Leo Durocher, over with the Giants, had finished 35½ games out of first place and he had a three-year contract, so why not Charley Dressen? "Because," said Walter F. O'Malley, who was doing a lot of juggling on mortgage payments and notes run up by previous Dodger administrations, "no one works in this organization except with a one-year contract."

Dressen enjoyed unparalleled newspaper backing. He was a tremendously cooperative little guy, good for stories in or out of the business. He had played quarterback for George Halas with the Decatur Staleys, fore-runners of the Chicago Bears, and was also one of the great check-grabbers of his day. He liked you, he fed you, usually with buckets of iced crab fingers flown in by some pal fresh from the waters off Vancouver Island. Dressen made a stand and O'Malley had Buzzy Bavasi, then one of his vice presidents, make a call to Alston.

Walt Alston had managed the Montreal farm club and had done well enough to move up to the head of the list of prospects in the event something happened in Brooklyn. "Get here as fast as you can," Bavasi advised Alston who was on the other end in his Darrtown, Ohio home, "but don't use your own name. Use that of Matt Burns."

The cover name which was provided Alston belonged to a lower-level employee of the Dodgers and represented totally unnecessary security. Alston could have gotten on that plane in Cincinnati wearing a Dodger uniform and no one would have known who he was. Or cared.

They hid him overnight and at the press conference the next morning all Hell broke loose. The Dodger offices were in Brooklyn's downtown business district. When the word got around on radio the people working nearby ran to the windows of their offices to stare across at the Dodger offices at 150 Montague Street as though there was a bomb planted in the lobby. It was a nippy November morning but the windows were flung up and people called to each other, demanding to know what was going on? Charley Dressen hadn't won the Series but hadn't he taken the Yankees to seven games in 1952 and six in 1953? What the club didn't need was a new manager. They'd do better to concentrate on getting another first-line pitcher.

And for crying out loud, this new guy, who was he? In a neighboring window a hastily crayoned sign materialized, one that made the front pages that afternoon—"Walt Who?"

Walter Emmons Alston had come up through the Cardinal system and managed for them after his playing days were done. He made the switch to the Brooklyn organization when Rickey moved from St. Louis, and worked his way up to one level below the top. En route he had been assigned the extremely sensitive task of managing Roy Campanella and Don Newcombe at their entry levels into the organized baseball system. They had come out of the Negro League for assignment to Nashua, New Hampshire, in the New England League. Alston was thirty-five, and he played alongside them, at first base as well as managing the club.

When the time came for the big move there were two candidates, Alston and Clay Hopper, who was managing the second of the Dodger's three Triple-A clubs at St. Paul. Fred Haney had the other one at Hollywood in the Pacific Coast League. Both Alston and Hopper were outstanding baseball men but Hopper was from the Deep South and had openly questioned Branch Rickey's bringing Jackie Robinson into the big leagues. Alston's section of Ohio hadn't exactly been a stop on the Underground Railroad, but if he had any thoughts about black players he kept them to himself. He got the job, and a one-year contract. Subsequently he got twenty-one more, a record in organized sports.

True, other men have managed a single club longer. There was Connie Mack in Philadelphia and John J. McGraw in New York with the Giants when they were the most important team in that city. Mack owned the club and McGraw, in with a lot of politicians and maneuverers, knew where most of the bodies were buried. In fact when McGraw quit because of illness he arrogated unto himself the right to pick his successor, a man he didn't particularly like but whose credentials were above reproach. Bill Terry, a .400 hitting first baseman, and the last .400 hitter in the National League, went on to win world championships with the Giants and find a place for himself in the Hall of Fame.

Alston's racial feelings? Well, that first year he straightened out Jackie Robinson. Robby was making probably twice what Alston was getting and knew it. He also knew that the customers came out to see him play, not Alston manage.

So Alston had a little meeting with Robinson and told him that the manager was the boss, and always would be and that if Robinson had any questions or didn't care for the arrangement he could either get out or they could settle it right there behind a closed door. Robby backed off. Ah ha? Alston's racial feelings surfacing after he had managed to repress them in his battle to the top, right? Wrong.

A year or two later he realized he had a couple of Hope Diamonds in Sandy Koufax and Don Drysdale. Goodness knows how many games they'd eventually win. Koufax won 165 in an injury-shortened career, 40 of them shutouts, four of them no-hitters, and is in the Hall of Fame. Drysdale won 209; he will eventually join Koufax if he can ever find time to lobby among the writers who cast their votes every January.

These young fellas were good and moreover, they knew it. And they took advantage of it in spring training at Vero Beach by treating the curfew hour in slightly cavalier fashion. What they found outside the fenced-in compound is questionable. Indian River County in the mid-fifties was not exactly Hollywood and Vine.

But they came in late, which was sinful, and proceeded to make a racket, which was stupid. Well, maybe not a racket. The wooden barracks, a hangover from World War II Naval Air Station days, had walls which allowed you to hear the next occupant clear his or her throat. Brave indeed was the Dodger who brought his wife to spring training and tried to live in holy matrimony.

Sandy and Don made the mistake of awakening Alston. He shuffled into his clogs and threw a bathrobe over his shorts. Then he clumped down the hallway to their room which had suddenly become as quiet as Forest Lawn.

"Open the door," demanded Alston. No answer. "Goddamn it, open this door," he shouted. Still no answer.

Alston swung a sledge-like fist at the door and splintered the thin paneling. Also he dislodged the big diamond in his World Series ring, most fortunate for the young stars because it distracted him momentarily. You might be burning to dismember a couple of young wise-asses infinitely more talented than you had ever hoped to be, but you pick up a loose diamond first. Especially if it belongs to you.

By the time he had recovered it and stuck it into his pocket, Alston's anger had subsided. Almost. "Listen," he said in a voice that sounded like someone's nail being drawn across a blackboard, "You do this again and I'll kill you. Both of you."

There's no record they ever tried it again. Since both were white, like Alston, the incident wiped out that whispered suggestion that the manager might be anti. Later in his career Jim Gilliam, finishing up as a player, became one of Alston's most trusted lieutenants and coach on the bases. Jim had come from the Baltimore Elite Giants, along with a pitcher, for the grand total of around $9,000.

Alston's path crossed that of Leo Durocher in 1954. The Giants beat the Dodgers by five games for the flag, and in 1955 the Dodgers won the pennant by 13½ over Charlie Grimm's Milwaukee Braves and 18½ over Leo's Giants. Then Leo was sent on his way by Horace Stoneham in favor of Bill Rigney, who had been undergoing training for the manager's role at Minneapolis, where the Giants had a Triple-A farm in the American Association.

Leo was out of baseball for a while and said he didn't mind, which of course he did. He was a big man on radio and on TV, giving it the gum-chewing routine as though he was in the third-base coaching box and giving the gin rummy routine at the Hillcrest Country Club, but that wasn't his long suit. Additionally his marriage to actress Laraine Day was starting to hit the shoals. Next thing baseball knew it was hearing Leo's sweeping accusation that there was an active blacklist against him. He called it "blackball," like in trying to get into some exclusive golf club.

"If it isn't a blackball," stormed Leo, "how come all those other guys are working and there's no job for me? Half them guys couldn't carry my jock."

Leo was right—about the ability of those guys to carry, etc. The owners looked at each other nervously, looked at Ford Frick, their commissioner, who looked back, then went into a huddle. Someone would have to take Leo.

He wound up on O'Malley's payroll in Los Angeles where fifty times as many people would recognize Leo if he walked down Sunset Boulevard (even though he'd be driving in a car with the top down exposing his shining noggin to the sun and smog) as would recognize Alston (who wouldn't be on Sunset Boulevard to begin with). Strangely, Leo proved an enthusiastic, able coach for Alston, minding his manners, steering his Hollywood chums away from the club house, aware of the pecking order. Until . . .

The Dodgers blew the third game of the 1962 playoff to Alvin Dark's San Francisco Giants. Alston's dugout strategy, with regard to his ninth-inning pitching, was not of the variety held up as an example for budding managers. All of a sudden there was a massive canceling of Los Angeles hotel reservations as the baseball world pointed toward San Francisco, four hundred miles to the north. Minutes after the game Leo's dam broke. "I can tell you one thing," he snorted, "We wouldn't have lost this one if I was managing this club."

Leo lasted a couple more seasons with the Dodgers but he might just as well have been the bat-rack as far as Alston was concerned. Then he left for Chicago in the mid-sixties where he almost won with the Cubs, left for Houston where the Latin ball players didn't know what in Hell he was talking about when he shouted, "Shut up, sit down, and listen" just as he had done at previous generations of ball players. In machine-gun Spanish they told him just what he could do, without assistance from anyone. Leo, pushing seventy, was pushed out of baseball by the same display of disrespect he had brought into the game as a Yankee rookie a half-century earlier.

Casey Stengel won the American League pennant every year in the fifties except those two he lost to Al Lopez, who had once worked for Stengel as a catcher in Boston. Lopez also went on to catch more games than anyone in the history of the game.

When he got into the World Series Stengel won every one in the fifties except in 1955 when he lost to Alston and in 1957, when he dropped a seven-game series to Fred Haney's Milwaukee Braves.

Haney, like Stengel, was a late bloomer. His playing career extended over a couple of decades and when it was over he started managing in Triple-A, worked up (or down) to the St. Louis Browns, pre-World War II. He didn't last too long and wound up in the minors again, which in those days was no big disgrace.

He got his second chance with the Pirates and from there moved to Milwaukee when the banjo-playing Charley Grimm was let go. All that talent seemed to jell at once in the beer capital. Haney had Hank Aaron and Eddie Mathews and Johnny Logan and Red Schoendienst and Del Crandall handling the catching and pitchers like Warren Spahn and Lew Burdette. The latter was a reformed kid window-breaker from Nitro, West Virginia, who was cut loose by the Yankees in 1951 partly in a trade for Johnny Sain and partly because he didn't quite fit the pin-striped concept. He repaid his favor by coming back and beating them three times in the World Series in 1957.

The next year Haney won in the National League again but this time the Yankees beat them.

There was to be one more splash. In 1959, the Dodgers made a tremendous recovery, coming all the way from seventh place the previous year. There was a tie at the end of the season and Los Angeles beat Milwaukee in a two-game playoff.

There are a couple other Hall of Famers who managed in the fifties who were well worth a call. Additionally they had been superstars before they managed. They were Frank Frisch and Rogers Hornsby.

Frisch was still playing when he was tapped for the managerial role in St. Louis. He inherited the Gas House Gang of the Dean boys, including Pepper Martin, famed for playing without an athletic supporter, and Ducky Medwick. He spent most of the forties in Pittsburgh. Then Frank finished up with the Cubs in the first couple years of the fifties. The Cubs weren't going anywhere following their last World Series effort in 1945.

Frank Frisch's interests extended far beyond the ball field. He was an ardent gardener, a voracious reader, an effervescent friend to most newsmen and radio people. Somewhere he's looking down at the nonsense of barring legit media from clubhouses an hour before a game, and roaring with laughter. Frisch would come out and drag you in and chew your ear. When he packed it in as a manager he went on to another career as a radio announcer covering the Giant games. He made famous the line "Oh, those bases on balls."

Everyone was familiar with Frisch's outside interests. One day in Ebbets Field, Red Barber, the Brooklyn broadcaster, pressed a novel on Frisch, insisting he read it. Standing by the dugout Barber enthused, "I can't remember when I enjoyed a book so much." Barber was a strong reader himself.

The book was *Quiet Street*, a novel by Zelda Popkin, which still surfaces occasionally. Frisch thanked Barber, took it and placed it alongside him on the dugout bench.

Now it was time for turning over the starting lineups to the umpires. Out came PeeWee Reese, the Dodger captain, in lieu of Burt Shotton (The elderly Shotton wore civvies, usually with a Dodger windbreaker and a fedora and this get-up was unacceptable on the field.). Bearing the other lineup card came Frisch.

As Frisch approached the men in blue his bile began to churn.

They were still working with three-man crews. This one consisted of Jocko Conlan, a Hall of Famer, Bill Stewart, who also officiated in high-league hockey, and Artie Gore.

Conlan had given Frisch the thumb the previous evening for pressing a point beyond what Conlan considered reasonable limitations. Frisch hadn't cared for the ejection and even after sleeping on it he started to seethe as though it had taken place only five minutes earlier.

As he turned in the card listing the order in which his humpties would hit (The Cubs finished a snappy seventh that season.) he muttered, "I hope we get a better game than the one you gave us last night."

Stewart was scheduled to work behind the plate. He had a New England accent and rabbit ears. "Y'routa the game" he yelled, giving Frisch the big motion.

Before departing Frisch unleashed his very best vocabulary. The officials stood around listening carefully, hoping he'd go beyond the usual invective so they could mention some unusual phrase or epithet in their report. Then he turned on his heel and strode into the dugout, en route to the banishment of the clubhouse. When you're thumbed out you can't stick around in view.

The first Cub batter took his stance against Preacher Roe, the angular lefty who was not above calling on a spitter when necessary. Bill Stewart called out to him to start pitching.

Suddenly there was a commotion off to one side. Something had come hurtling out of the Cub dugout in the general direction of home plate. What's this? A book? The batboy ran across, picked it up, and turned it over so Stewart could read the title: *Quiet Street.*

The same could never have happened with Rogers Hornsby when he was managing because the Rajah was far from a book man. He was a .400 hitter (several times) and he saved his eyes for baseball. Books weren't the only things he brushed off. Hornsby stayed away from movies for the same reason.

Rog wasn't above reading the newspaper, though not to check

on what was happening in Hoover's Washington, but how they made out at Belmont, or Arlington Park, or Santa Anita. He was one of the bigger bettors on horses in baseball, going back to when he was probably the highest-priced star in the National League in the twenties.

Hornsby blew a lot on the horses. He was once called on the carpet by Commissioner K. M. Landis who demanded to know whether Hornsby was betting on horses, forbidden fruit in baseball at that time.

"Goddam right I do," he stormed, "And I pay off a hundred cents on a dollar, too."

Hornsby's last job was with the first-year Mets. He was into his sixties and Stengel hired him partly as a favor and partly to see whether some of Hornsby's hitting ability might rub off on his collection of kids, misfits, re-treads, and psychopaths. (Name one other major league club where the first baseman had an arrest record for having exposed himself to young girls.) The experiment failed, of course. Hornsby's steely blue eyes could still pick up a pitch as well as anyone who ever lived. He demonstrated it with his batting practice shots, big belly and all.

But he couldn't teach someone else how it was done. It can't be passed along as Ted Williams, who had a similar talent, discovered when he tried managing and instructing the rag-tag Washington Senators club.

The Hornsby name had tremendous glamor. He never lacked for a job although he had to work occasionally in the minors, and he once ran a recreation program for the City of Chicago which had become home for the one-time Texas farm boy. But Hornsby had shots in the majors managing with the Cardinals, the Braves, the Cubs and twice with the Browns and never could claim he had not had a chance.

In the early fifties the moribund Reds were casting around for help. Johnny Neun, famous for having executed a triple play unassisted when he was a first baseman with the Tigers, had replaced Deacon Bill McKechnie and was in turn replaced by Bucky Walters, a big pitching hero with the Reds. Walters couldn't do it and they went for Luke Sewell, who had the club for a couple of years. A change was dictated and Hornsby was available. Maybe because of some of his hitting ability.

It was the old story, but by this time Hornsby's attitudes had hardened to the point where he wouldn't even bother going out to the mound to take the pitcher out. He'd simply climb to the top step of the dugout and beckon the unfortunate with one finger, leaving him to cringe his way off the field. How many grievances would be filed by today's crop of millionaire pitchers against this treatment?

Nor was this the ultimate. Hornsby would never let the shelled pitcher depart for the merciful isolation of the clubhouse. No sir, sit right down here alongside me and watch the rest of this game. Not that Hornsby would say a word to him, or even indicate he was aware of his being there.

After it was over, the Reds losing another, you could get your clothes off and maybe in that hot shower you might wash away some of that humiliation for a while anyway. Tomorrow could always be another day.

Except for one thing. Hornsby always showered along with his players, a holdover from the days when he was one himself. One afternoon some beaten pitcher was showering but not enjoying it particularly because whenever he'd close his eyes, then open them he'd see Hornsby's bulldog visage alongside him under the next shower. The pitcher happened to glance down and promptly made a standing broadjump effort of perhaps five feet directly to his right and away from his manager. And for an excellent reason. The manager, busy with the lather on his head and shoulders, was nonchalantly urinating on his losing pitcher's leg. No question about it. The shower head would have to have been defective in five places to produce an errant stream like the one he felt playing on his leg. The pitcher might have been a loser but he was smart enough to distinguish between hot water and piss.

Hastily he got out of the shower, dressed, and made his way up to the Reds' offices in tired old Crosley Field. He sought out Gabe Paul, the club's general manager.

"Mr. Paul," he blurted, "y'gotta stop him."

"Stop who?" asked Paul.

"You gotta stop the manager. He was just pissing on me in the shower."

Gabe was right in the middle of a season in which the Reds were to wind up a dreary sixth, with no pitcher able to win more than a dozen games. His road secretary had just checked the turnstiles for that day's game and had come up with a snappy 4,781 customers.

"What," he asked, "would you like me to do?"

5

We Got You in Bronze

ALPHABETICALLY, the stars of the fifties elected to the Hall of Fame were Yogi Berra, Lou Boudreau, Roy Campanella, Roberto Clemente, Joe DiMaggio ('51 was his last year), Bob Feller, Whitey Ford, Monte Irvin, Ralph Kiner, Sandy Koufax, Bob Lemon, Mickey Mantle, Eddie Mathews, Stan Musial, Robin Roberts, Jackie Robinson, Warren Spahn, Ted Williams, and Early Wynn. Additionally, fifties managers Casey Stengel and Al Lopez made it along with fifties umpire Jocko Conlan, a bantam out of Chicago who knew a lot of people who were subsequently exterminated in gang wars or by the FBI. And then, of course, there was the dour Yankee empire-builder, George Martin Weiss, the general manager.

In this group Williams and Wynn could claim their playing careers extended across four decades. To come up with this impressive span a little gimmick is called for. You have to start at the end of one decade and finish up at the beginning of another. For example, Mickey Vernon was legit (1939–60) and

Minnie Minoso wasn't. Bill Veeck brought him back as a coach in '77 with the White Sox, had him play a game just for the record. That gave him the four decades. There have been others in baseball able to claim this unusual distinction, but not many. There was Eddie Collins, a Hall of Fame second baseman of an earlier era. Five decades? Right here, a Washington pitcher by the name of Nick Altrock.

Altrock began in 1898 and hung around, largely through friendship with Clark Griffith, until 1933 when he finally packed it in and became a coach. There's no Altrockian niche in the Hall of Fame, and won't be. Not with an 84–75 mark.

Altrock developed a penchant for pantomime and later he teamed up with Al Schacht, another Washington pitcher, and they toured post-season, barnstorming as a clown act. The act is best remembered by Schacht's having worked in a frock coat and top hat with baseball pants. After a while Al got into an argument with Altrock and they went through their entire routine without talking to one another for years. It sounds like the groundwork for a bad TV play.

Clown stuff was big in the fifties not only in the minors where the tastes might be a little less sophisticated but in the majors as well. A big favorite was a one-time minor league pitcher, Max Patkin, who was also a contortionist.

The Hall of Famers elected to date from the fifties can't stir much criticism. It's going to be tougher for the players of that era who haven't made it so far. They include men like the Yankees' Phil Rizzuto; Detroit's George Kell; and Johnny Mize, who starred for the Cards, Giants, and Yankees. Twenty years after they've finished they are no longer eligible via the writers' annual balloting. They are moved along to the veterans committee, whose broader scope includes all of baseball going back to the 1880s, plus the shadowy area of the Negro leagues. (What we know about that league now is mostly hearsay.) All of this makes it a lot tougher, especially since friendships and pressures occasionally intrude into the veterans committee's considerations.

There is a definite syndrome in baseball not listed in any

medical literature, called the Hall of Fame syndrome. Its onset
comes usually in middle-age or later and it cuts former stars
down to size. Players who would walk right past a newsman
assigned to report about him 154 games a year suddenly remember not only his name, but his wife's name twenty years
later. How about the time Casey got that real good load on at the
World Series party and got up on the table to make that speech,
heh-heh?

Here he comes, rushing across the crowded room, hand extended in greeting, some enchanted evening during an old-timers'
gathering, saying things like, "Remember the time we were in
Sacramento and all the Yankees were in the bus after the game
with the local team; that spring when we trained in Phoenix and
we had guys like Yogi and DiMaggio and Reynolds and Raschi
and Lopat, and Mickey was the only rookie in the bus? Spec
Shea called the kid over to ask him who the best baseball player
was in the whole world and the kid answered Joe Marty. Heh-
heh. Sure were some great old days."

The syndrome obliterates the "what's-in-it-for-me?" attitude
that went with a twenty-game season or a .320 batting average.
The old-timer says, "Hell, there sure were a lot of laughs in
them days, weren't there, heh-heh? You guys gonna vote on the
Hall of Fame this year and how does that balloting work
anyway?" As if he didn't know.

The Hall of Fame is the highest accolade in the sport. The
player who insists it doesn't matter because it doesn't put a
nickel into his pocket is just plain lying.

There are a number of items laid out for voting guidance but
most go by performance and contribution to the game. There's
something in there about character or setting an example to the
youth of the nation, but all that tends to become a wry gag.
Some of the men in the Hall of Fame would have humped a
wolverine in their day before going to the ball park, given the
opportunity. Others followed the precept that whiskey will spoil
once it's uncorked so you'd better not leave any. Another group
specialized in staying up all night trying to cheat a little at stud
or gin.

In the end the writer is mostly influenced by his relationship to the person for whom he's voting. Good guy? Yes. Bad guy? No. Bad guy with qualities secretly admired by Walter Mitty? Maybe. Lots of sweating palms around mid-January when the Baseball Writers Association starts counting the ballots because your name has to appear on three-quarters of those cast to make it. Adding to the difficulty is the qualification laid down among the writers for voting.

Active baseball writers are eligible, along with ten-year (life-time) members. There aren't too many of the latter and they get fewer each year. Young fellows don't stick around for ten years of baseball writing any more. And the young fellows are liable to ask, Enos Slaughter? Who was he? Walker Cooper? Never heard of him.

The actual Hall of Fame story has been told dozens of times. You'll find the details every summer in the where-to-go section of the Sunday paper. Makes a good two-day trip and is good wholesome entertainment for the entire family, etc. Make your reservations at the nearby motels well in advance.

There are a few facts worth underlining. Baseball's Hall of Fame was the first in sports. The idea was first thought of by Ford Frick, in the mid-thirties, when he was president of the National League. He got the idea from the Hall of Fame for Great Americans on the campus of New York University.

Wouldn't it be a little presumptuous putting ball players in the same done-in-bronze category as Washington, Lincoln, Jefferson, Edison, and the Wright Brothers? They'd give it a chance, but where?

Up in Cooperstown, N.Y., in the heart of Deerslayer country, there was a gentleman named Stephen Clark who had a great deal of money and a hankering after a baseball museum to go along with several other local museums. A quantity of old baseballs and old baseball gloves of indeterminate age was discovered around the countryside. There was also a discredited report, although official, by a duly appointed commission back in the early 1900s, that Abner Doubleday, a Civil War general, invented baseball around Cooperstown. Errant nonsense.

What we know as baseball originated as the British game of rounders and there were all kinds of printed references to it a hundred years earlier than 1839. But Jim Farley, FDR's postmaster general, an old semi-pro first baseman and a life-long fan, went along with the gag and issued a commemorative stamp for the centennial in 1939. After that there were thousands streaming to the scene every summer to catch the annual inductions and watch an exhibition game between a couple of major-league clubs. Which was a good idea since Cooperstown is one of the more pleasant parts of our country.

And it was such a good idea that the other sports started imitating it. Pro football set up in Canton, Ohio; basketball in Springfield where Dr. Naismith first installed the peach baskets in the local Y; hockey in Toronto; racing in Saratoga; swimming in Ft. Lauderdale; college football in Kings Island; Ohio, etc.

The Yankees of the early fifties have been treated here earlier. After their five-series sweep, 1949 through 1953, the club figured out that twelve players, four coaches, Casey Stengel, and trainer Gus Mauch, had been party to this momentous feat and called attention to it publicly. Only one of the players was to be a Hall of Famer, Yogi Berra, a three-times MVP in the decade.

Among the coaches Bill Dickey had been inducted previously. Stengel moved in after his managing days were over. Stengel's days in uniform ended when he broke a hip in mid-season, 1965. They hustled him into the Hall of Fame the following year in a special election which acknowledged the hazards of old age, Stengel's in particular. He outfoxed them and went on to enjoy his Hall of Fame mantle for nine additional years.

The dozen Yankee players who were responsible for all those five Series were: Hank Bauer, outfield; Bobby Brown, third base; Jerry Coleman, second base; Joe Collins, first base/outfield; Ed Lopat, pitcher; Johnny Mize, first base; Vic Raschi, pitcher; Allie Reynolds, pitcher; Phil Rizzuto, shortstop; Charlie Silvera, catcher; and Gene Woodling, outfield. Coaches were Dickey, Frank Crosetti, Ralph Houk, and Jim Turner, the latter ruling the pitching with an iron hand and a little black book.

Since the names of Berra and Brown are linked in the same paragraph, the well-worn roommates story might as well be turned over again. They had brought Berra up from Newark at the end of 1946. In 1947 he was taking his turn catching regularly. He was a gnome-like apparition who could hit any kind of pitch with ferocious enthusiasm and was also able to block just about anything—ball or runner—at the plate.

They roomed Yogi with Brown, a pre-med student who later would become a cardiologist in Texas as well as part-owner of the Texas Rangers. When they went on the road they took their books. With Brown it was medical books, big heavy ones. With Yogi a load of current comics made for easier toting.

They were reading themselves to sleep one night and by a strange bit of timing they both decided that they had had enough at the same moment. Yogi flipped the last page of his comic book, grinned with pleasure, and put it aside just as Brown closed his three-pound *Materia Medica*. Yogi smiled satisfiedly across at his chisel-featured roommate.

"Mine was great," he said. "How'd yours come out?"

6

Was He *Really* the Best?

THERE ARE CERTAIN ITEMS in baseball directly traceable to some particular person's desk, doorstep or pitching rubber. More than a hundred years ago Candy Cummings discovered that if you held the ball a certain way when you threw it, the gosh-darned thing actually curved. A half-century later Christy Mathewson noticed that if you made a certain move with your elbow while throwing the ball, it curved the *other* way.

Further up the line Branch Rickey put numbers on the backs of players' uniforms in St. Louis and thirty years later planted protective fibre caps on the skulls of his Pittsburgh Pirates. Rickey had a piece of the company which manufactured the caps but on the way to the bank he also happened to save a few careers and possibly a few lives.

Harry M. Stevens, the concessions boss, invented the "hot dog" when it became apparent he wasn't going to sell too much soda pop to Polo Grounds customers on a forty-degree day in April. Ford Frick, the third commissioner, invented the Hall of Fame, admittedly cribbing the idea from the Hall of Fame for Famous Americans which he had visited on the campus of New York University as a newsman. Frick was on his way up through the ranks of baseball's executive levels and when he wondered, "Why not famous baseball players?" a sufficient number of listeners paid attention.

No one knows who invented baseball's Most Valuable Player Awards. There are MVPs in virtually every sport today but it was a baseball first, starting back in 1923 as an official tribute, with cash to match. Ten years earlier the Chalmers auto people gave an open touring car to the player rated best in each league but the complimentary-car practice was dropped after four years. Ty Cobb, Tris Speaker, Eddie Collins, Walter Johnson, Larry Doyle, Jake Daubert, and Johnny Evers were some of those who got a complimentary ride.

George Sisler, a .400 hitter with the St. Louis Browns, was the first of the official MVPs, followed by Babe Ruth in 1923. The National League got into the act the following year when it was Walter Johnson in the American League and Dazzy Vance, the Dodger pitcher of indeterminate age and interchangeable name, as the first of the National League winners. Dazzy's name, according to his Hall of Fame plaque, was "Arthur C.," but veteran Brooklyn writers always called him "Clarence." The "Dazzy" came from his ability to dazzle the hitters, just like Cy Young's name came from "Cyclone," because in no way could Denton True Young work out to "Cy."

When Dazzy won the MVP it carried more than merely honors and a headline some time during the off-season. The league gave a one-thousand-dollar prize, in gold. Fred Lieb, then president of the baseball writers, recalls making the presentation to Dazzy at Ebbets Field. Fred lived across from the Polo Grounds and, like most New Yorkers of his day, used public transportation. The day he had to go out to Brooklyn to give Dazzy his sack of gold coins he took the elevated train down to mid-town, transferred to the Brooklyn subway for a total investment of ten cents and rode to the Ebbets Field stop, all the time the gold resting in his lap.

"I just sat there and let people think it was my lunch," explained Lieb. "Today you'd have Wells Fargo assisting Brinks."

Eventually the writers took over the balloting. The doubloons stopped and were replaced by a fancy plaque. When Mickey Mantle was selected unanimously in the American League in 1956 he received a solid gold coronet, but it wasn't directly for his MVP. Mickey had won the Triple Crown (most homers, highest batting average, most RBIs) that year. A free swinging bunch in Baltimore, which had just come back into the majors, threw the darndest party and stuck the crown on his head as the King of Swat. It will be remembered that Babe Ruth was originally from Baltimore. Mickey was the only Triple-Crown winner in the fifties and only one of eleven in all of baseball.

Phil Rizzuto, the little Yankee shortstop who was MVP in 1950, had a similar experience. That year Phil also won the Hickok Award, put up by the Rochester belt people, and it was really something. There was seven or eight thousand in gold in the buckle, and a few additional thousands in the gems which studded it.

Phil did what every right thinking athlete of his day would have done. He picked two of the most impressive jewels for rings for Cora and himself and turned the rest of the material over to the nearest goldsmith for melting.

In today's era of quarter-of-a-million a year players it's possible a winning athlete might keep the buckle to adorn a den alcove. Or might not.

The Hickok Award, incidentally, was not only for baseball but for all pro sports. That year Rizzuto was rated superior to Stan Musial, Jim Konstanty, Ted Williams, Ezzard Charles the heavyweight champ, Ted Lindsay the hockey superstar, Ben Hogan, Indy winner Johnny Parsons, and Hall of Fame jockeys Eddie Arcaro and Ted (the Slasher) Atkinson. Rizzuto has never made the Hall of Fame for some unfathomable reason, and in spite of the fact that he was highly visible as a TV announcer during most of his prescribed twenty years of eligibility.

Little Phil's memorable performance in 1950 (he hit .324 and made the Yankees virtually waterproof in the infield) helped set a Yankee keynote for the entire decade. They won the flag eight times in ten tries, and won six World Series. Over in the National League Brooklyn was the closest with five pennants and two World Series.

In both these cases of obvious superiority a single performer provided his particular club with a tremendous lift. Yogi Berra won the MVP title three times as did his opposite number with the Dodgers, Roy Campanella. Both, of course, reside in the Hall of Fame.

Mantle won in successive years, 1956 and 1957. Mantle's 1956 election was unanimous, a profound achievement which had been accomplished three years earlier by Cleveland's third baseman, Al Rosen.

Before Rosen, little Bobby Shantz, a lefthanded pitcher, managed to win twenty-four victories for a fourth-place Athletics club.

Shantz filled old Connie Mack Stadium in Philadelphia every time he pitched. His efforts kept the club in town perhaps a year or two longer before it began moving around the country. He accounted for thirty percent of his team's victories in 1952. Fans would leave New York on evening commuter trains to Philadelphia, grabbing a sandwich en route, just to see him pitch.

Shantz had a small problem. He liked to hit, too. He was up there crowding the plate a bit in a meaningless game at the end of the season when he was nailed on the wrist of his throwing hand. He was never the same, although four or five years later, when the Yankees got him, as they did most of the good talent of the era, Bobby was still able to contribute in several successful pennant races.

Shantz was an odd little guy, only 5 feet 6½ inches tall, weighing 140 pounds. He believed there was something to pitching besides getting the ball past the hitter. He was probably as good a fielding pitcher as any, and when he pounced on a bunt he did it with the grace of a ballet dancer. He literally dared the best of them to lay it down to either side. His whirling throw to second base to set a double play in motion was worth the price of admission.

Baseball was not his only athletic pastime. He also loved swimming. It may sound peculiar but a Yankee management which didn't particularly worry about where its stars spent their post-game hours, and with whom, got all worked up at the thought that Bobbie might be risking a game to spend an afternoon swimming and diving. The Yankees management was a suspicious lot; when people in towns on the road hospitably invited the Yankee players to use their pools they could think only of ulterior motives. Like over-chlorination, or under-dressed bathing beauties.

Casey Stengel couldn't have cared less how Shantz got ready to pitch. However, Jim Turner did. Jim Turner was the guy Casey had hired early in his career as Yankee manager to be in charge of pitching. Turner was a taciturn, suspicious Tennessean, who had been a big-league hurler with the Braves. "Here," Casey said to him. "You run it."

Turner did. He always carried a little notebook which he constantly examined with pursed lips. Turner was tough looking, and tough, thanks to a career in which he had pitched fourteen years in the minors before becoming a twenty-game winner with a 1937 Boston club that finished fifth. No one was going to tell Jim Turner what was good, or what wasn't, for pitchers. He didn't like daytime swimming before a night game.

"Look at me," Shantz used to say anxiously after being applauded for a dive off the high board at someone's fancy country-club pool, "Am I getting sunburned?" Little Bobby could handle Stengel, but he didn't want to tangle with Turner.

Al Rosen, now a Yankee executive, was the best Jewish player in the fifties. Like Shantz, he won the MVP without being on a winning team. Rosen was a Southern collegian who didn't take too many steps backwards, and his multi-fractured nose (college boxing and a few arguments) stopped a lot of racial nonsense on the field before it got started. In his big year he had a .336 batting average and led the league with forty-three homers and

145 RBIs. Today he'd command a quarter-million dollar salary.

The following year Rosen played most of the season with a broken finger literally sticking out of his glove and up and away from his grasp when he held the bat. He still hit .300 that season, probably a nine-fingered record. The Indians won 111 games, beat the Yankees by eight full games, and ended the Yankee dominance after five successive World Series triumphs. That's a record, too.

Shantz and Rosen weren't the only players who won MVP during the fifties without being on a winning team. In '52, Shantz's year, the National League winner was big Hank Sauer, who had moved from Cincinnati to the Cubs to play in the outfield. He hit a modest .270, but his twenty-seven homers and 121 RBIs led the league. He led the MVP voting by a shade over Robin Roberts, the righthander who had a 28–7 mark with the Phillies that year.

Old timers still talk about that ballot. It was unusual in that one of the electors didn't have Roberts on his ballot at all, leading observers to wonder what he was looking at from his perch in the press box? It turned out that the errant elector was (a) a Philadelphia newsman who had himself pitched for the Phillies in an earlier era and (b) no particular admirer of Roberts to the point where he brushed him in their daily comings and goings. Roberts of course went on to make the Hall of Fame but he never got close again in the MVP voting.

One of Berra's three MVPs came in 1954, the year his club bowed to the omnipotent Indians. Jackie Jensen, of Boston, won in 1958, even though his team finished thirteen games behind the Yankees, and Ernie Banks, another Hall of Famer, won in '58 and '59, with clubs that finished fifth both years. Ernie used to greet everyone with "It's a great day for playing a ball game" (the Cubs are the only no-lights team in the majors) and more than one listener wondered what precisely did he mean?

In 1958 Jackie Jensen won the MVP in the American League, hitting .286 for the third-place Boston Red Sox, hitting thirty-five homers and driving in 122 runs. Mantle had dipped to .304, with a league-leading forty-two homers but Jensen won the honors even though his teammate, Ted Williams, led the league with a .328 batting average well below his lifetime average of .344.

It's reasonable to assume Jensen will never forget his victory. Neither will the writer. As one of the electors (three from each league city and please cast your ballot in the interval between the end of the regular season and the start of the World Series), I was required to line up my choices, one to ten. On my ballot Jensen didn't show up, and there was a lot of flat-A conversational and media fuss around Boston when it came out. My defense, of course, was sound, but meaningless to the hyenas around Fenway Park.

I had simply voted for Bob Turley of the Yankees (He got seven votes to nine for Jensen.) and then I went on to nine other players, all of whom I deemed superior to the eventual winner. Moreover, I didn't see the need of consulting any of my colleagues with a nervous, "Who you voting for?" since I had put in a lot of press-box time that season.

Ted Williams placed seventh. Any time the batting champ of the league finishes that far down, the nuts start coming out of the woodwork. "Investigatory reporting" followed. The ballots are supposed to be secret but two writers voted him tenth and one voted him a ninth, and it all leaked out. Discussing this with a loose-tongued colleague the additional question surfaced, "And who could have been so stupid as to leave Jackie Jensen off the ballot entirely?" "Me," I replied, "And if you get out your pencil and write down these names I'll tell you why." I then proceeded to tick off the names of Pete Runnels, Frank Malzone, and Ted Williams.

"Those," I offered, "were the men in my opinion who did more for the Red Sox against the Yankees than any others on their club. And that's the only yardstick I can use with any honesty. I can only go by what I've seen. (As a Yankee regular correspondent I had covered 98 percent of their 154 games that year.) I've done the same with the other clubs the Yankees played and after

I got through sifting them I made my pick. And now I thank you one and all."

This got into my chum's column. Jensen made a point of snubbing me the various times he saw me in 1959. The opposing pitchers snubbed him, in turn. He didn't get a single vote in the balloting following his big year.

I wasn't anti-anyone who wasn't a Yankee, even though it could have looked that way. When Yogi Berra won it for a third time in 1955, Gil McDougald's name topped my ballot. I forget what his accomplishments were that year but I remember Stengel saying he could never have won it, two games behind, with two weeks to play, without McDougald. He didn't say the same thing about Yogi.

And what Stengel said about McDougald had to come from the heart because Gil was no particular favorite. Stengel liked them to play when hurt ("Y'got the uniform on, aintcha?") and McDougald absolutely refused to do it with a hand injury that was a balky healer. It looked ready to go and the Yankees could have used his bat, but McDougald stubbornly refused to play until he thought it was well.

The decade closed in the American League with Nelly Fox, the White Sox second baseman, winning the title. He was the catalyzing force in the first White Sox flag in forty years. Fox was bigger than he looked, 160 pounds, 5 feet 10 inches, but that perpetual plug of tobacco wadding out his jaw oddly made him look smaller and tougher. He was about as good a bat-handler as there was in the league and when the White Sox played the Dodgers and lost in the World Series, Fox batted .375. He played almost twenty years in the big leagues, lived another ten after he hung them up before succumbing to cancer.

In the National League Brooklyn won five pennants during the decade, and had four MVPs. Roy Campanella accounted for three, winning on alternate years, 1951 through 1955. Don Newcombe, a twenty-seven-game winner, won in 1956.

Campanella easily qualified as the player most entitled to rail against his misfortune. In the 1957–1958 off-season, when the

Dodgers were making their transition to the West Coast and some of the big salaries were starting, Campanella was the victim of an automobile accident on an icy night. It put him in a wheel chair for life.

The other Hall of Famer who figured in the National League balloting in the fifties was Ernie Banks, the Cubs' good-cheer ambassador who won in 1958 and 1959 despite a second-division finish by Chicago both years.

One sociological aspect of the game is brought into vivid focus by the MVP balloting in the fifties. The National League obviously went all-out to tap the available black talent; the American League simply dragged its feet. The Red Sox were the worst, but as late as 1952 a Yankee scout, prodded in conversation by Campanella's initial successes, blurted, "We have no policy on Negro players," meaning of course, "We're not signing them."

One or two clubs, notably Cleveland and St. Louis under Bill Veeck, went after the black players but the rest pretty much dawdled, although Washington had for years been using black players under the guise of Latins. It gave the National League an edge which the American League spent the next fifteen or twenty years trying to blunt.

Only two of the National League's ten MVP ballots in the fifties resulted in white players being named. Jim Konstanty, the remarkable reliever who drew the Phillies' starting assignment against the Yankees for their 1950 World Series, won the honors that year. In 1952 Hank Sauer, who batted .270 for the Cubs with thirty-seven homers astounded everyone, including himself, by slipping through as the winner. Robin Roberts, Hall of Fame righthander who won twenty-eight games for the Phillies that season, twice as many as anyone on his club, should have been the winner but one of the Philly writers, an old pitcher himself, was feuding with Roberts and pointedly left him off his ballot completely.

Sauer, Roberts, and Joe Black, the Dodger reliever who used to unnerve the opposition by throwing his warm-up pitches from a yard back of the rubber, split all but one of the first-place votes among themselves, 8, 7, 8 and finished 1-2-3. Behind them came Hoyt Wilhelm, the knuckleballer who was to pitch more relief innings than anyone in history (1,870), Stan Musial, Enos Slaughter, Jackie Robinson, PeeWee Reese, Roy Campanella, and Red Schoendienst. So Hank Sauer, a super nice fellow but no particular super star, can relate to his grandchildren about the year he won MVP and finished ahead of four Hall of Famers.

After 1952 it was Campanella, Willie Mays, big Newcombe, home-run king Henry Aaron, and Ernie Banks. Campanella and Banks were later voted into the Hall of Fame and Mays joined them in 1979. Aaron is ticketed for early inclusion.

Balloting for the MVP is intensely subjective, which is just another way of saying that prejudices usually run the show. Nice guys don't finish last; sometimes they finish higher than they should. And over in the veterans' committee, a twelve-man group considering players no longer eligible under the writers rules, likes and dislikes bubble very close to the surface. Ernie Lombardi, who probably hit a baseball as hard as anyone who lived, went to his grave unhonored by inclusion because he once got into the wine at a party in Cincinnati where he was catching at the time and announced that the club general manager was a cheapskate for refusing him a one-thousand-dollar raise. It got back, and the gentlemen held it against big, goodhearted Ernie for the rest of his unhappy life.

Well, is there a solution? Give the players the vote? Players build friendships and dislikes, too, and are perhaps a little more gullible when a con job is being pulled than newsmen.

The public? How about the time they stuffed the ballot boxes in Cincinnati on the All-Star game so that seven or eight Reds starters made the National League's batting order an embarrassment? That was a "public" effort, endorsed by the community.

Administrators and brass? Please, they don't even know how to handle their own help.

Obviously the writers are stuck with it. But they can always say that any mistake came from the head or heart but never from the wallet. The pay for this service at season's end is one big zilch. That, plus a little heartburn when called upon to defend your picks.

7

Casey Stengel's Vaseline Pot

USING YEAR-END STATISTICS and standings as a means of measurement, the best single-season team of the 1950s was the Cleveland Indians club which beat the Yankees for the 1954 flag by eight full games. Then they fell flat on their faces and lost four straight to the New York Giants in the World Series, but that's another story.

The Indians won a startling 111 games, still an American League record, and the strong impression lingers that it was done mostly with pitching. Bob Lemon and Early Wynn, both subsequent Hall of Famers, won twenty-three games each; Mike Garcia won nineteen, Art Houtteman, fifteen, and a twilighting Bob Feller, thirteen. Lemon's and Wynn's victories were tops for the league; Garcia was the earned-run leader.

The hitting was good, not great. Bob Avila won the batting title with a .341; Al Rosen, who hit .300, did so with a busted index finger on his throwing hand. Larry Doby led the league with thirty-two homers. The Indians followed that hoary baseball maxim, which can be applied to all competitive sports: hold your own with the good ones and murder the stiffs.

They beat the Boston Red Sox, twenty of twenty-two times, and won nineteen games from Baltimore, providing the Orioles with a dubious first-year present following their switch from St. Louis.

In New York, Casey Stengel had enjoyed a run of five straight pennants and five straight World Series victories, beginning in 1949. He had beaten the Dodgers three times, the Phillies once, and the Giants once. But he had never won a hundred games in a season. This time he won 103, and it got him nowhere, except second place.

Stengel demonstrated all kinds of ambivalence in his feelings toward the Indians. Al Lopez, their manager, who caught more games than anyone in the history of the majors, was his kind of guy. Lopez had missed playing with Stengel by a couple of years but he caught for him when Casey was shepherding the dreary Braves during a couple of pre-World War II years.

They were close. Matter of fact the only times Stengel was beaten for the American League flag after he had taken over the Yankees it was Lopez who did it, once with the Indians and again with the 1959 White Sox.

Casey didn't care for Cleveland as a 1954 pennant contender. Over a drink he'd question sharply the ability of its players, a rarity for him. He had watched the Tribe get off to a slow start, then climb into the lead by the second week in May. He waited in vain for them to drop off. His Yankees played them even or better all through the season but when the Indians faced the rest of the league they were invincible and Stengel showed his irritation.

"We'll get 'em, don't worry," he vowed in July and again in August, "them guys ain't gonna slip me no vaseline pot," a baseball expression which has yet to show up in Bartlett's Quotations.

There was something about Cleveland that bothered him. It might have been the whispers about its possible shadow ownership, but Stengel was no child. One of his own owners, Del Webb, knew and did business with lots of Las Vegas people, some of whom had records which weren't cut by Frank Sinatra or Benny Goodman.

In five years with the Yankees Casey had averaged 97.4 victories per season and had left everyone for dead. Here he was on his way to his first one-hundred-victory season and he was on a treadmill with cement-soled shoes. It was an old ball player's nightmare.

It was getting down to the September short strokes and the Yankees played a pair in Chicago previous to going into Cleveland for a final mid-month doubleheader. Paul Richards had the White Sox and he could squeeze a lot out of his pitching. There was a split with the Yankees losing one game in ten innings after they had been within an out of taking it in regulation.

Stengel was now six behind but that didn't phase him, at least outwardly. Being that far behind with the Yankees was something, but Stengel had known bigger gaps in previous managerial roles, major and minor. And adversity was nothing new.

The Yankees bumped over on sleepers from Chicago and arrived to find Cleveland, particularly their hotel, the Hotel Cleveland, crawling with Indians' fans. They had arrived the previous night and by 10 a.m. they had practically worn out the elevators. Jimmy Cannon, the columnist, made the mistake of going up to his room to brush his teeth before breakfast and wound up inhaling his ham and eggs more than an hour later. He couldn't get on an elevator. "The hotel," announced Cannon, "is out of control."

Stengel gave the impression of being completely in control. "Don't worry," he advised at breakfast, "We're six behind, right? We beat them two here today and we're only four behind, right? Then we go get 'em."

Wrong. Before a record crowd of 86,563 the Indians beat them twice. Whitey Ford's shoulder tightened up in the first game when it was tied one to one in the sixth. He had to come out for Allie Reynolds, who lost it via three additional Indian runs in the last two innings. The immense crowd howled its approval.

People had come from all over Ohio and the abutting states, and had brought their beer with them, internally and externally. The record is still in the book for a regular season game. (The Dodgers drew three straight crowds of more than 90,000 in the cock-eyed shaped Los Angeles Coliseum against the White Sox in the 1959 World Series.) In the book the record is 84,587. The rest were workers, newspaper people, etc., all of whom were clocked through the turnstiles.

In the fifties one of the favorite arguments among newsmen was whether or not to use the paid figure or the over-all figure in stories. One of those supporting the over-all number pointed out effectively, "If they dropped an atom bomb on the joint, would it get everyone or just those who had bought tickets?"

The Cleveland crowd was there to see the Yankees crushed, exterminated. A hasty shiver ran through the stands in the opening inning of the second game when Andy Carey doubled, Mantle struck out trying to bunt and Yogi slapped one into the right field seats off Early Wynn. This gave the Yankees a two to nothing lead.

The shiver communicated itself to Wynn, too. He twitched his heavy shoulders, glared at the next hitter, took an enormous breath and seemingly forgot to exhale. He stood out there on the mound all puffed up like a poisoned snake. And then he proceeded to pitch like one the rest of the way.

Not another Yankee got a hit until Hank Bauer scratched a successful bunt leading off the sixth. And there was nothing after that. Before Yogi had gotten his homer Wynn had fanned a couple. Now he fanned ten more.

With that kind of pitching all he needed was a big inning and he got one on four hits good for three runs. They came in the fifth off lefthander Tommy Byrne. Now, instead of the expected four games behind, the Yankees were eight behind leaving town. And they still had to slip out of town.

It wasn't easy. Thanks to a phobia on the part of general manager, George Weiss, against airplanes the Yankees traveled exclusively by train. In the late fifties they set some kind of a record for spending two nights on a train from Washington to Kansas City, a trip that required three hours by air. Weiss's attitude was all the more difficult to comprehend because he had survived almost by a miracle the wreck of the Twentieth Century Limited early in his career of running a minor league club.

The Yankees' special cars, due to haul them over to Detroit, were sitting on a siding. The Cleveland terminal was crawling with semi-drunken celebrants trying to track down the trains that would take them home where they would be able to tell their less fortunate friends what they had missed. There had been no TV broadcast of this awesome event; although sold out the Indians turned down a seventy-five-thousand-dollar fee, big money in those days.

The double-loss wasn't the Yankees' only setback. After the game a special dining room for a steak meal had been reserved. The players hadn't eaten since the morning. The food was fine, the surroundings lavish except for one minor defect; no air conditioning and no windows to open.

Casey was further mortified when he tuned in the conversation of a number of the writers and the club's road secretary. He discovered they were making other plans. With the Yankees out of it their offices had advised that they pick up other clubs. One or two were told to stick around and cover Cleveland for a while. In the trade it was known as "band-wagoning," meaning the writers jumped on the band-wagon of the winners down the stretch. As Stengel boarded he looked around and said with a combination of bewilderment and resignation, "I guess I'm losing my writers too."

The Yankees completed their road trip, went home and finished the season before small crowds rattling around cavernous Yankee Stadium. The big attraction in town was over at the Polo Grounds where Leo Durocher's Giants were whipping along to a National League pennant and what was to prove an incredible sweep of the Indians in a four-game World Series.

In the final weekend they dreamed up a couple of stunts

calculated to attract a few extra customers. On the final Saturday they honored eighteen men who had participated in all five World Series victories, 1949 through 1953.

The next day Casey dreamed up a "power" lineup for a final game with the A's. He sat down his lighter-hitting infielders, put Yogi on third, Mickey at short (his original position in the minors), Bill Skowron on second, etc. They faced the A's and a righthander, Art Ditmar, who had a zero and four record.

The A's beat them, eight to six. It was that kind of a year for the Yankees.

8

You Mean *Nobody* Got a Hit?

THE ODDS ON A NO-HIT GAME unfolding before your eyes are pretty far out. In a century of National League pitching there has only been a handful more than a hundred. The American League's three-quarters of a century has produced perhaps eighty. The local computer, the one that occasionally figures out you are seven million dollars overdrawn on your personal checking account can probably figure out the odds if you want to look into it further.

But what are the odds on some pitcher having two in a single season? Or two of them pulling off the same trick in the same season, same league? That's how the American League started the fifties in the no-hit department. It had ten during the decade and four were traceable to Allie Reynolds and Virgil Trucks, early on, as they say on TV.

Reynolds's Creek Indian ancestry gave him a look of brooding malevolence out there on the mound and it also gave him a few extra points toward the end when he was just lobbing it in instead of scorching someone's eyebrows. He won 182 regular season games, plus seven for the Yankees in the World Series. He has been skipped over in Hall of Fame balloting and if he makes it to Cooperstown now it will have to be via the Veterans Committee. Other aspirants won more games than Reynolds but he can claim a first over the rest of his contemporaries, that is, he was the first American League player-representative at a time when going to the mat with the owners involved a lot more risk than it does today.

Allie came to the Yankees from Cleveland shortly after World War II. In July 1951 he beat his old team with a no-hitter, then treated the Red Sox in September in the same way. The Red Sox game was made memorable by one of Yogi's infrequent errors on a pop foul. With two away and Ted Williams at bat Yogi circled, then dropped one that would have meant the ball game.

Reynolds' impassive look never changed. He cranked up, delivered, Williams swung. Again a pop foul. This time Yogi caught it and held on. An oddity about Allie's feat was that a sore elbow had kept him from throwing all through spring training. Oh yes, Yogi's explanation for dropping the foul: "It got into an air pocket."

Virgil Trucks was an Alabaman whose career pretty much paralleled that of Reynolds, although Trucks' original team, Detroit, didn't offer the same opportunities for World Series play that the Yankees did. The most unusual business about Trucks' two no-hit jobs in 1951 was they comprised two-fifths of all the games he won that season. Around his ultimate five victories he managed to sprinkle nineteen losses. When Casey Stengel had all those pitchers losing twenty or more games with the early New York Mets he used to say, "Y'gotta be a good pitcher to lose twenty games in a season," the meaning of which was obvious. Trucks missed Casey's yardstick by one game.

His first no-hitter was against Washington, no big deal. Then he treated the Yankees in similar fashion late in August at a time when the defending champs were engaged in a desperate battle with the Indians for first place. In comparison to the dead-serious Reynolds, Trucks was considered "fun-loving" and there was at least one American League city from which he was barred during his career under pain of a summons.

The Dodgers provided the National League with the only double no-hit pitcher in the fifties, Carl Erskine. The dandy little Hoosier righthander beat the Cubs in Ebbets Field in 1952, then treated the New York Giants in similar fashion in Brooklyn four years later.

Erskine's second no-hitter was a comparative yawn, stacked against the excitement generated by his first. He pitched the first one with a three-quarter of an hour delay in the middle caused by a rainstorm. When the game resumed he had a sizeable egg-shaped bump on his head.

"We played cards during the rainstorm," recalled Erskine. "Hodges, PeeWee, Jackie Robinson and me, and every once in a while we'd have someone check on how the weather was doing. We had a pretty good lead in the game and we didn't want to lose it to the weather.

"The old Ebbets Field clubhouse used to be down in a kind of basement. Twenty feet up toward the ceiling there were windows hung so that they'd swing out to let the air in. No air-conditioned club houses in those days. You wanted some air you climbed a ladder and opened a window.

"The window was open but you couldn't tell whether it was still raining. So I put my cards down and climbed up and looked out. I hit my head against the metal corner of this big window and saw stars. I darned near fell off. But the rain had stopped and about ten minutes later we were back on the field."

Waiting along with the players had been a weekday afternoon crowd of 7,732, including five hundred Knothole kids, and five hundred blind people.

Oddly, the only man to get on base for the Cubs was their pitcher, Willie (the Knuck) Ramsdell. His nickname came from his complete dependence on the knuckle-ball. His regular name, Jess Willard Ramsdell, indicated someone had been an admirer of the former heavyweight champ who lost the title to Jack Dempsey.

In those days the Dodgers used to have a post-game TV show

called "Talk to the Stars." The stars talked for fifty dollars a shot. The producer of the show used to pick the respective heroes of each side and usher them into a tiny booth, post-game.

Ramsdell had given way to a replacement when the Cubs pinch-hit for him. But he was very much interested in seeing whether his old Dodger teammate, Erskine, was going to make it, and he stood watching from the dugout runway. The producer approached and advised that if Erskine finished up pitching a no-hitter Ramsdell would be the Cubs "hero" for having gotten the walk. "Great" said Willie.

Then he turned to the business at hand. There were two away, only one out to go and Eddie Miksis, another of the Dodgers who had long been traded to the Cubs, was at the plate. "C'mon Carl," shouted Ramsdell to Erskine from the runway, "You can strike this bum out."

Erskine did, but not before Ramsdell sweated a bit. Erskine ran it up to a full count before Miksis grounded out.

Six others pitched no-hitters in the National League in the fifties besides Erskine. Vern Bickford, of Boston, opened with a victory over Brooklyn in 1950 and Harvey Haddix, a Pittsburgh lefthander, closed it with one against Milwaukee in 1959.

Haddix's was more than a no-hitter. It was a perfect game for twelve innings and then a loss. In the thirteenth, an error, sacrifice and an intentional walk was followed by the only hit off Haddix, a double by Joe Adcock. It is listed among the perfect games having nine or more innings during the fifties. The other such game was Don Larsen's in which he beat the Dodgers in the 1956 World Series.

Back to regulation no-hitters. After Bickford came Cliff Chambers, of Pittsburgh, who beat the Braves in 1951. In 1954 there was Jim Wilson, of the Braves, who won over the Phillies. Sam Jones, of the Cubs, famous for pitching with a toothpick stuck between his teeth at all times, triumphed over Pittsburgh in 1955 and in 1956 Erskine's second no-hitter was followed by a Cincinnati performance involving three pitchers against Milwaukee. Johnny Klippstein, Hershel Freeman, and Joe Black, the former Dodger, took it through the regulation nine innings, then Black lost it in the eleventh.

Finally, Sal Maglie, who had moved from the Giants to the Dodgers, came through with one against the Phillies in 1956, and that wraps up the National League story in this department except for a backward glance at Vern Bickford.

Vern Bickford was a craggy, slow-talking Kentuckian who learned his trade the hard way. He was only a nineteen-year-old kid when he played in the Mountain State League. Standard pay then was sixty dollars a month and all you could eat on two-dollars-a-day meal money. Stan Musial was the Mountain State's most famous graduate. He started in Williamson, West Virginia, where he had to be discouraged by a wise and seasoned old manager from sneaking over to the bus station and beating it back home to Donora, Pennsylvania.

Helping to keep Musial going were carefully spaced five-dollar bills mailed to him by his parents, plus an occasional home-cooked meal which they brought to him on his father's one day off from the job at the wire mill where he hustled hundred-pound bales of wire onto freight cars. The following year Musial got the same sixty dollars a month but moved up a modest notch; shortly thereafter he was a major-league star.

Unlike Musial, Bickford spent four years playing for Welch where he lit up no skies with a virtually break-even record as a righthander. Then Uncle Sam relieved him of the monotony with a three-year stretch in the U.S. Army. When he came out the Braves had him at Hartford, then at Jackson, Mississippi, where he was still pretty much break-even.

In 1948 they brought him up to the majors where he won eleven in the drive that brought Boston its first flag since the Miracle Braves of '14. It was obvious that he had a lot of talent, largely self-developed. In 1950 Bickford won nineteen games, completed more games than any other National League pitcher, and pulled a no-hitter against Brooklyn in an August night game at old Braves Field out by the Charles River.

Bickford was twenty-eight when he came up to the majors. He

had left a good deal of his stamina down there riding all-night busses and inhaling grits. He only lasted into the 1954 season. Fate was to deal him a cruel blow. He died of cancer before he was forty.

Bob Feller actually pitched the first American League no-hitter of the fifties, beating Detroit twelve days before Allie Reynolds pitched the first of his two that year. For Feller it was his third. Three was a major-league record until Sandy Koufax came along to boost it to four in the sixties. Nolan Ryan tied it in the seventies.

Navy service took a big bite out of Feller's career, just how much no one can really judge, but it was a big one. Before his three years in service he had averaged better than twenty-five victories a year for three successive seasons.

He was into his last big year (twenty-two victories) when he pitched his final no-hitter and although he was still a member of the Indians staff when they lost four straight to the New York Giants in 1954 he failed to make an appearance in that World Series. And in the 1948 Series against the Braves Feller was charged with two losses.

He won a lot of other games, however, 266 of them. It's reasonable to assume he'd have been an easy three-hundred-game winner if he hadn't spent those three years in service. One of the thrilling sights in the early fifties was Feller swaggering in to relieve as the Indians played their trump card in a game they deemed vital to win.

No-hit efforts by Boston's Mel Parnell in 1956, Chicago's Bob Keegan in 1957, and by Detroit's Jim Bunning in 1958 were standard professional jobs, but there were a pair of weird ones rounding out the picture. In 1953 Alvah (Bobo) Holloman made his first major league start for the moribund St. Louis Browns and pitched a no-hitter against the Athletics on a damp spring night. Don't look for Holloman in any Hall of Fame niche. His entire major-league career is encompassed in a single "won three-lost seven" line in the Baseball Encyclopedia. He came and went like the figment of a fevered sports writer's imagination.

The rainy afternoon of Bobo's epic event hadn't been much around St. Louis. The Browns couldn't make up their minds whether to call the game or not. Bill Veeck, dying on the vine with an eighth place ball club that was to lose one hundred games, figured he had nothing to lose playing. He'd have those thousand or so die-hard customers who despised the more affluent Cardinals, who once had been merely tenants at Sportsman's Park.

So Holloman, who figured he'd have a night off, suddenly found himself with a ball in his hand and eventual national recognition. To get a little mileage out of this feat Veeck announced anyone who had been brave enough to come to the park that night was entitled to another free ride. Stubs from the no-hitter would be honored at any future Browns game. Why not? There were all kinds of empty seats available in the Browns' last year in St. Louis, even when they were playing the contenders like Cleveland, the Yankees, or Detroit. That was the year the Browns, or rather Bill Veeck, had Eddie Gaedel, a three-foot, seven-inch, sixty-five-pound midget lead off against Detroit on a Sunday afternoon.

Veeck had a gun ready to nail Gaedel if he dared to swing. He walked, and left the game for a pinch-hitter. Forever. But he's in the record book. He's also on the Cincinnati police records for being picked up in the downtown area drunk late one night. Asked for his occupation, Gaedel ignored his real calling, that of a vaudevillian and announced, "Major league baseball player."

The Yankees were the victims of the last American League no-hitter pitched in the fifties; they were tamed by Hoyt Wilhelm's knuckle-ball. Wilhelm was having a sour year (three and ten) with two clubs. Cleveland had traded him to Baltimore and he caught the Yankees on a lackadaisical Saturday afternoon with the pennant already wrapped up, and quickly clinched his final victory.

He ran through them in one hour and forty-eight minutes, facing one extra batter. It was raining at the end of the game. It was also the end of a long, losing season, for the Orioles pennant contender was still a few years away. They drew a third of Memorial Stadium's capacity, ten thousand for Wilhelm's no-hitter and it so inspired the populace that a grand total of four thousand showed up the following afternoon for the final Yankee appearance in Baltimore that year.

9

Pardon Me, Boy, Is That the Chattanooga Choo-Choo?

THE FIFTIES proved the most significant decade in the game's history in travel. It started with the clubs on trains and St. Louis as the Western outpost. It ended with both major leagues whizzing back and forth from sea to shining sea, trying to make time-zone adjustments and learning what it was like to arrive at an airport at 3 a.m. with no cabs.

Baseball travel began shortly after the Civil War. Clubs like the Cincinnati Red Stockings moved around in wooden railroad cars, three-tiered for sleeping, and lit by whale-oil lamps. As things progressed schedules were formulated based on train travel. Ball clubs were always favored customers of the railroads and invariably received special treatment. Their special cars would be hooked on the back of crack trains like the Twentieth Century Limited, the Broadway Limited, the Congressional, and the Yankee Clipper. The Southwestern Limited, the New York to St. Louis train, picked up a ball club after a day game in New York, left after supper and deposited its charges in St. Louis late the next afternoon. No one complained about things being so slow.

Then the planes came in after World War II, first those uncomfortable, solid, and slow-moving DC-3s. They had been service workhorses, and with two-and-one seating across they could barely accommodate an entire ball club. You entered on a short staircase on the side toward the tail and struggled up a steeply inclined aisle toward your seat.

Things improved with the DC-6s. and Constellations, which were used on the coast-to-coast hops without having to refuel. Then the jets arrived in the final couple of years of the fifties and suddenly there was no concept of distance between places, only time.

Larry MacPhail of the Yankees and the late father of the president of the American League was the first to use planes. He flew the Yankees to St. Louis for a series in the late forties. The correspondents along were whipped into such a froth that they datelined their stories, "St. Louis, Via Special DC-3," just like Charles Lindbergh. After all it was only twenty years since Lindbergh had executed his memorable New York to Paris flight.

A year or two after this event the Dodgers got into the flying picture by leasing a plane from Eastern Air Lines. Shortly thereafter the Dodgers flew just about everywhere, hauling their players, the press, radio commentators, and assorted friends of the management. Walter O'Malley moved right along with the times, going from a DC-4 to an Electra, and then into jets. He maintained his own flying crews, and rented out the plane to other clubs for their hops. All Dodger planes have been called Kay-O, in honor of O'Malley's wife, Kay.

Further back the Dodgers had another plane which was more or less for the personal use of Branch Rickey, then president of the club. Rickey was a one-fourth owner and was forced out by O'Malley at the start of the fifties.

Rickey, one of the true geniuses of the game, combined his talents in an odd way on the Dodgers. He would make the top-level decisions, then go scooting off to look at some lefthander half-way across the country, frequently landing on a dirt runway to do it. He'd be here and gone five minutes later, forgetful of his toiletries, his hat, and even his socks, all of which he managed to borrow, along with tipping money, from Dodger employees or friends, both of which were in abundance.

Particularly the employees. At one time the Dodgers had twenty-three farm clubs, including three at the Triple-A level, which is presumed to be the step below the majors today.

There was a post-season event called the Junior World Series, which brought together the champions of the American Association and the International League, and there really was nothing "junior" about it. A winning club in the Junior World Series would probably acquit itself credibly in the majors today.

In 1948 the St. Paul Club of the American Association played Montreal of the International League. Both were Dodger farms. They had a third Triple-A farm at Hollywood in the Pacific Coast league. The only comparable performance had been six years earlier when the Yankees had their Kansas City farm (American Association) play their Newark, New Jersey (International League) farm. It's a pretty safe bet the personnel of any of these four clubs could easily break even in the majors today.

Once Rickey was buzzing along to an important meeting in the Midwest. (He once confided that he could have made a good president, and he meant of the United States, not a baseball club, and that he had never attended an unimportant meeting.) He looked up from his reports. They were going to be late.

Then his chief pilot came back and advised that they couldn't get into Cedar Rapids but that he was going to try to land in Des Moines instead where Mr. Rickey could take a train.

Rickey was vexed. He had given his word he would be on hand.

No chance? The pilot, a World War II combat flier, compressed his lips into a thin line. "Sorry, not a chance Mr. Rickey. Not in this stuff. It'll have to be Des Moines."

Rickey pursed his lips, thoughtfully. Then he brightened. "Look," he said, "try to get into Cedar Rapids somehow. I'll take the responsibility."

On today's twenty-six clubs there are probably a good percentage of players who have never spent a night sleeping on a train. Little things like getting up in the middle of the night and having to raise the bed in the narrow compartment to be able to use the toilet are joys they'll never know. There were other pleasures too, like the time Leo Durocher played gin rummy all the way from New York to Milwaukee and then tried to keep the game going when the Giants got to their hotel.

Now even the short hops, two, three or four hours, by train are gone. There's no more Detroit-Cleveland, Milwaukee-Chicago, New York-Philadelphia, Boston-New York.

There aren't trains anymore, for one thing. For another, door-to-door bus travel is wonderfully convenient, literally a road-secretary's dream. Two busses usually do it, one for the players, one for the media, etc. All the gear, baggage, etc., go into the bins in the belly of the bus. You can't beat that.

In the fifties though, baseball travel by train was something special. Terminals in the heart of town bustled; there were people saying hello and goodbye; a train departure was subtly dramatic.

In the scratchy dawn, players climbed off unshaven, hustled by cab to the hotel, gulped a big breakfast, read the local sports pages quickly, then tried to grab a few hours of shut-eye before an afternoon game.

On a night-game on get-away day, the railroads would defy U.S. postal regulations about tardiness. The train would be held up on one pretext or another, and the engineer would be cursing softly up front with watch in hand. Here they'd finally come, the old ones, the young ones, the drunk ones, and the sober ones, laughing and shouting as they sprinted along. The conductor would then put his heirloom Hamilton back into his vest which his grandfather had worn and accept, with just the shadow of a nod, the hundred-dollar bill proffered by someone like the

Charles Walter (Chuck) Dressen, new manager of the Dodgers, signs his contract as Walter O'Malley, club president, looks on.

Casey Stengel gives some
pointers to second
baseman Bobby
Richardson.

on Larson pitches to last man up in his World Series perfect game. (Below) George Weiss, Yankee general manager, gives an earful to Casey Stengel, Yankee manager.

Hank Aaron (left), Eddie Mathews (center), and Joe Adcock (right) at Yankee Stadium prior to opening game of 1957 World Series. (Courtesy of the National Baseball Hall of Fame and Museum Inc.) (Below) Ernie Banks receives congratulations from Dale Long (8) and batboy. Umpire is Tom Gorman. (Courtesy of the National Baseball Hall of Fame and Museum Inc.)

Ted Williams being interviewed in Washington by broadcaster Bob Wolff. (Courtesy of the National Baseball Hall of Fame and Museum Inc.)

Roy Campanella completes circuit on home run and receives congratulations from Jackie Robinson (42) and batboy, while umpire Dusty Boggess watches. (Courtesy of the National Baseball Hall of Fame and Museum Inc.)

Nellie Fox, White Sox second baseman. (Courtesy of the National Baseball Hall of Fame and Museum Inc.)

Willie Mays and Horace Stoneham, owner of Giants at the time. (Courtesy of the National Baseball Hall of Fame and Museum Inc.)

Stan Musial making his 3000th hit at Chicago, May 13, 1958. (Courtesy of the National Baseball Hall of Fame and Museum Inc.)

Al Kaline, outfield and first baseman for the Detroit Tigers. (Courtesy of the National Baseball Hall of Fame and Museum Inc.)

Milwaukee Braves' pitcher, Warren
Spahn. (Courtesy of the National
Baseball Hall of Fame and Museum Inc.)

Hall of Famer Yogi Berra
(left) and Whitey Ford,
pitcher for the Yankees.
(Courtesy of the National
Baseball Hall of Fame and
Museum Inc.)

Braves' Duffy Lewis or the Giants' Eddie Brannick. Then away everyone would chug for Cincinnati, or Detroit, or St. Louis shouting, "Whose got the cards?" or "Did someone pick up a late paper?"

Railroads appreciated ball club business because they knew in April what to expect in September. Also the clubs paid their bills on time.

A great many railroad people were baseball fans, particularly the dining car and club car personnel. Nothing was too good for someone who had just collected a couple of homers or who had pitched a big game. The rest of the club rode along on the hero's coat-tails. Stewards on dining cars remembered first names and there'd be an extra couple of those little bottles of booze for after-dining relaxing.

Drinking on trains was sometimes a problem, sometimes a laugh, like the year the Yankees trained in Phoenix because millionaire-builder Del Webb wanted to show his world champs to his neighbors. In the middle of spring training in 1951 they left on a two-week tour of the West Coast to shake a little money out of the natives who saw nothing in those days but Triple-A ball or less. It was the Los Angeles Angels and the Hollywood Stars in Los Angeles, the San Francisco Seals and the Oakland Oaks in the Bay area.

Big Yankee attractions that year were Joe DiMaggio, representing the Old Guard; Phil Rizzuto, MVP the previous year; the pitchers Vic Raschi, Allie Reynolds, and Ed Lopat; and a bunch of newcomers ticketed for stardom, Mickey Mantle, Gil McDougald, and Billy Martin.

The road secretary made a slight miscalculation in closing down the press room at the old Adams Hotel, which was headquarters. There were a couple of bottles already started and since he had to get down to the depot early he suggested that a couple of newspapermen take care of them.

Ordinarily this wouldn't have been much of a problem except it wasn't ordinary whiskey but some Greek brandy, the gift of Jim Londos, the world wrestling champion who had settled down to promoting wrestling matches in Phoenix and who was supremely grateful to have some of his old friends around. The newspapermen, applying themselves diligently, didn't leave any bottles other than empty, and barely made it down to the Southern Pacific depot, where strong arms boosted them aboard.

One made it to his bunk, all right, the other found some additional spirits which caused his one good eye to twinkle in anticipation. (The other was glass, like what he had in his hand.) A couple of drinks and he, too, was gone. A couple of outfielders managed to catch him before he toppled to the compartment's carpet.

They hauled him down the corridor and deposited him with the road secretary. A reasonably kind fellow, he put his accounts aside and shoved the writer into the lower berth, eventually climbing into the upper.

The train arrived in due course in Los Angeles and the revived writer thanked him for his trouble. Then he added, "The next time you put a fellow with a glass eye to bed, though, make sure you take out the glass eye."

"I would have," replied the road secretary, "except that in your condition I wouldn't have been able to tell the difference."

Mornings were pretty bleak on baseball trains but the evening meal after a big day game was a social highlight. Have Mickey Mantle hit three out of the park or Willie Mays go four for four, or Stan Musial or Ted Williams put on a special show and you could invariably count on some trimmings. After whispered consultation between the road secretary, whose duties sometimes ranged from that of a Senior Patrol Leader to a St. Bernard, and the dining car steward, the vintage grape would appear and the steaks would take on an added dimension.

With the Dodgers dining car service the few times they rode the rails was an undiluted joy. With Jackie Robinson, Roy Campanella, and Don Newcombe, stars shining brightly, the dining car employees would unlock the larder and toss the key down the next embankment. Anything you wanted in the way of extra portions.

Robinson's presence was electric even in the fifties after the sensation of his being the first black man in major league ball had become a matter of everyday life. Once on a run up from St. Louis to Chicago on the Wabash, the train stopped at Decatur, Illinois, home of the original Chicago Bears who had been born as the Decatur Staleys, and Charlie Dressen was explaining to anyone who cared to listen that he had once played quarterback for the Decatur Staleys along with a lot of college guys who had played under assumed names and had trusted George Halas not to renege on his arrangement of twenty-five and fifty bucks a game. It was true; Little Cholly was a pro quarterback, all five feet, seven and one-half inches of him.

It was dark in the station but suddenly the Dodger party was aware that the station was filled with people, several hundred of them, just standing there. No one said a word, but everyone looked at Robinson, who was seated by a window, the shade down. Wordlessly, Robinson raised the shade and waved. A cheer went up. He waved again. No speeches, no handshaking. After a while the train got moving. An older writer, who had traveled a generation earlier with the Yankees, announced, "Haven't seen anything like this since Babe Ruth used to go through. There was a difference though. The Babe would get off and walk up and down the station to collect a crowd."

On the same Wabash run, which had a high rating on the eating scale, we were once treated to an interesting bit of dining. Among the writers was a fellow with a pretty good reputation for being extra handy with the knife and fork. The repast that evening on the Bluebird tested him, but he surmounted all hurdles.

As he pushed back he announced, "That was great. I'll bet I can eat another meal just like that one."

To the road secretary, who had a guarantee of a certain number of meals to be met, anyway, this was not a challenge to let slip by. "I'll buy you another meal, Herbie, but you'll have to promise to eat it all. Okay?"

They shook hands and five minutes after polishing off the

cherries jubilee our hero was back into the shrimp cocktail, the mock turtle soup, the steak, etc. He made it, all right, but when the Bluebird arrived in Chicago it carried one slightly over-stuffed and slightly thoughtful baseball writer.

"Wasn't Herbie great?" marveled one observer, "being able to go around twice on a meal like that?"

"No," retorted the other. "He cheated. He didn't eat the rolls the second time around."

The Yankees once played their way back across the country and when they got to Dallas at dawn the late great Dizzy Dean was waiting for them at the platform with a string of Cadillacs, attended by a bunch of smiling millionaire-Texans, who couldn't be mistaken for chauffeurs by any stretch of the imagination. Diz had moved to Texas and had been bragging to his new neighbors about his Yankee pals. (After his playing days he had served briefly as a Yankee broadcaster.) So they got together and had a large breakfast lined up for the conquering heros, who were scheduled to play a spring exhibition game in Dallas. There were items not ordinarily seen on hotel or lunch-room menus like country ham and red-eye gravy.

Dizzy was all over the place, urging everyone to dig in (at 7 o'clock in the morning, no less). After the heaps of food had begun to disappear he made the rounds with cigars asking everyone how he had liked it? "Great," exclaimed a city fellow, "I'll admit it was a little unusual eating chicken so early in the morning but I can't remember when I had chicken that good."

"Chicken!" yelled Dizzy. "That was pheasant, dammit, and I shot it out of season just for you guys."

On another Texas trip there was an evening to kill after a Dodger stop in Fort Worth where they had a farm club. This could have been Vin Scully's first year with the club because I remember him as a member of a party going to the movies before making the train.

The choices weren't numerous. It was either *Winchester 75* (the original one made in 1950 with Jimmy Stewart) or *Hamlet* (the one with Sir Laurence Olivier and Jean Simmons).

The lines for the shoot-'em-up stretched down the street. Admission to *Hamlet* was no problem and in we went.

Shakespeare was pretty good on the eternal verities but he sure didn't know too much about train schedules. Hamlet and Laertes were just getting warmed up in the final big sword-play scene when one of us looked at his watch.

"My God, we only have ten minutes to make the train!"

We jumped up, ran out of the theatre to the sound of clashing swords, and puffed to the depot, a block away. We clambered aboard, settled down, gasping.

Finally one of us, later to become a nationally known columnist, said, "Damn, I'll never know how that one came out."

"Don't worry," offered a companion with literary pretensions, "There were no winners."

10

Four in a Game

THE HALL OF FAME IN COOPERSTOWN offers no special niche for one-time performers, those who have had that one big day, then are forgotten. Don Larsen is the only pitcher ever to fashion a perfect game (no one gets on base) in the World Series, but the only way he'll ever get into the Hall is to pay his way at the box office or have them send him a pass good any time.

It's the same for Johnny Vander Meer, the only man ever to pitch a couple of no-hitters back to back. Vandy hurled for the Reds before and after World War II, was a strikeout artist, and the book shows him with more successive no-hit innings than any other—twenty-one and two-thirds. He went into his no-hitter against the Boston Braves June 11, 1938 with one-third of an inning from a previous game, added that second no-hitter in the first night game ever played in Brooklyn four days later, and then went three and one-third innings in his next game against the Braves before giving up a three-and-two hit through the box by Debs Garms, a truly impressive performance. He's in the record book, but not the Hall of Fame where there are items like consistency, longevity, etc., as factors.

In the same boat are sluggers Pat Seerey, Joe Adcock, and Rocky Colavito, all of whom connected for four homers in a game.

Four in a game is quite a trick. Ten men have done it and of this group only Lou Gehrig, the famed Yankee Iron Horse and Ed Delahanty, a Philly Nationals slugger of the nineties are in that pantheon.

Of this distinguished group, oddly enough, three came through in the 1950s. They were Gil Hodges of the Dodgers, Adcock, playing for Milwaukee, and Colavito, when he was a favorite in Cleveland. Since then Willie Mays made it in 1961 and among contemporary players it's been Mike Schmidt of the Phillies in 1976. Ruth never did it, nor Hank Aaron, Ted Williams, Jimmie Foxx, and all those other super-sluggers.

Hodges wound up his career with 370 homers. The four he nailed that August 1950 night against the Braves in Ebbets Field had a few extra grace-notes. For one thing he got a pair off a brace of very good pitchers, Warren Spahn and a youthful Johnny Antonelli. The others were off a pair of journeymen, Norman Roy and Bob Hall.

Braves manager at the time was Billy Southworth and he must have had other things on his mind when he started the lefthanded Spahn in Ebbets Field with its chronic array of righthanded sluggers and its short left field porch. Antonelli was just a kid at the time, destined to go on and become an outstanding pitcher with the Giants.

Hodges also had other things on his mind. He had just become a father a second time. The small apartment he and his wife and their first child were occupying in Flatbush had suddenly become a lot smaller. He needed a larger apartment. (Ultimately he was to settle for a house on a quiet street in Brooklyn where he lived right up to the time he died while managing the Mets a decade and a half later.)

The writers, asking questions about Gil's muscular feat,

wanted to talk about his hitting but Gil kept asking whether anyone knew of any apartments that could ease his problem? One of the local morning papers came up with the cute headline, describing his situation: Hits Four in One, Needs One for Four. When Adcock executed his four-homers job four years later in Ebbets Field the Braves had moved to Milwaukee. They had also adopted the fibre protective batting helmet as standard equipment. Charley Grimm, the manager, had made sure his men wore them. By wearing one, Adcock stuck around to savor his feat.

On a Saturday afternoon Adcock stroked a homer off big Don Newcombe, a double and a homer off Erv Palica, a third homer off Pete Wojey, and finished up with a ninth-inning swat off Johnny Podres, then a nineteen-year-old leftie out of Witherbee, New York, who little dreamed he'd be the winning pitcher in the deciding game which would bring Brooklyn its first—and last—World Series crown the following hear.

The following afternoon the Braves were off and running again against the Dodgers. Adcock took a toe-hold and tried to drive one into the seats. Clem Labine caught him on the side of the helmet with a brush-back pitch which struck with such force it dented the helmet. They carried the big slugger off on a stretcher but he revived and went on to play another dozen years in the big leagues and wind up with the commendable figure of 336 home runs.

Rocky Colavito's four homers for Cleveland in June of 1959 was the final such effort of the decade. He clouted them in Baltimore's Memorial Stadium, no particular haven for a home-run hitter. (The entire American League had accounted for fifty-seven homers in that park the previous year.) Colavito's came in succession, the first off Jerry Walker, then two off Arnie Portocarrero, a big kid who, like Colavito, hailed originally from the Bronx section of New York City, and finally a wrap-up rap off Ernie Johnson.

There is an entertaining footnote to the four-in-a-game and it involves Gehrig, who belted a total of 493 before disease cut him down in his prime. Gehrig's four-in-one were against the Athletics in Philadelphia, June 3, 1932 and it was the first such effort in the twentieth century. His, too, came in succession. The first three off George Earnshaw, one of Connie Mack's World Series heroes, the last off Roy (Popeye) Mahaffey.

Back in New York that same afternoon there was a monumental changing of the guard. An ailing John J. McGraw who had guided major league baseball teams for more than three decades, had decided to pass the Giants portfolio along to his first baseman, Bill Terry. There was never any love lost between this pair but McGraw, a baseball man to the very core, recognized ability on the field and off.

There was no full-dress press conference with the cocktails, the hors d'oeuvres, the floodlights, or the silly talk. There was a simple bulletin-board announcement in the clubhouse, where few reporters snooped in those days.

One of the writers, whose afternoon paper had plenty of editions left that day, spotted it, rushed to a phone, and delivered several thousand words on the event, right off the top of his head. He gave 100 percent on this particular effort because he knew that the stepping-down of John J. McGraw called for an exclusive front page headline.

He was wrong, although it was scarcely his fault, as the split headline which greeted him later attested: "Gehrig Hits Four; McGraw Resigns."

11

Doing the Continental

THE WINDS OF CHANGE blew steadily through the fifties, sometimes reaching gale proportions. There were a succession of
franchise switches in the first half of the decade—Boston to
Milwaukee, St. Louis to Baltimore, Philadelphia to Kansas
City—which seemed monumental at the time but which actually
took a back seat to the big going Coast-to-Coast moves.

The players expanded their sphere of influence beyond their
most exotic dreams, or those of the owners. What started as one
or two minor differences shortly after World War II later gave
birth to a Players Association with check-off dues, full-time legal
aid, and a director who, through favorable court decisions, has
emerged as the most powerful figure in the game.

The owners' collective asininity speeded up the pace of the
players' urge to organize. Also the post-war climate was favorable toward a change in the traditional boss-worker relationship.
Changes had taken place in people's thinking, perhaps as a
result of so many people going to war. On their return to

"normal life" their horizons had broadened. In baseball, it turned out there was a great big world out there beyond the centerfield fence.

A free-lance organizer named Robert Murphy suddenly appeared on the scene right after the war talking "union." He seemingly had no backing, no address, no phone number, operated out of his hat, and was available at a moment's notice. His initial target (and, as it turned out, his only one) was Pittsburgh with its strong union sentiment, thanks to the supporting coal and steel industries. A number of the Pittsburgh players had strong union-family connections; one or two of them had lost relatives in mining accidents. They gave Murphy an attentive ear.

So did enough others in the club so that one late afternoon, they decided that there'd be no Pittsburgh team out there on Forbes Field to play the Dodgers that evening unless they had a written agreement to their demands which today would seem ridiculously innocuous. You know, things like laundry money, meal money after a night game, and spring training travel allowances. There was none of the big stuff which was to come later and divert millions into the pockets of the players and their lawyers and agents.

Hall of Famer Frankie Frisch managed the club in Pittsburgh. Frisch was a surprisingly cultivated person despite his Gashouse Gang exterior. He was an avid reader, a horticulturist, and above all a firm believer that there was nothing more important in the world than baseball. To Frisch it was inconceivable that a player would even give the right time to some outsider trying to talk him out of playing as a means of having his demands met. He felt you could always ask for concessions on the day the boss's hemorrhoids were bothering him less than usual. For a lifetime .316 hitter like Frisch of course the boss, any boss, invariably could manage a smile.

But the Pirates of '46 weren't all .300 hitters. They listened to union organizer Murphy, decided to sit down right then and there. What about the crowd gathering in the twilight? It could go fry.

A pitcher named Truett (Rip) Sewell saved the day for the owners. A fiery Alabaman with a quick tongue, he jumped on a bench, commanded everyone's attention, and proceeded to turn things around by his scorn directed at "quitters" who would listen to "outsiders." Maybe the "outsiders" had other motives beyond the welfare of the players. The mutinous cadre dissolved, the Pirates took the field, Murphy vanished into the night and was never heard of—or seen—again. He was a Harvard man and very few Harvard men wind up in cement, but every once in a while someone wonders what actually happened to him.

Sewell received an expensive watch as a year-end gift from an appreciative Happy Chandler, who had just taken over as commissioner. He saved Happy a lot of grief and it stalled the organizing schedule a few seasons.

But as the fifties dawned the players slowly put their organization together, this time without the help of any outsiders. People like Ralph Kiner, of the Pirates and Allie Reynolds, of the Yankees, were voted league representatives and empowered to talk with the owners at the league meetings. You couldn't ask for men with better credentials. Kiner was seven-times National League homer champion. Allie had pitched a couple of no-hitters in '51 and was a key figure in the Yankees' five straight World Series triumphs.

To the astonishment of most, this pair was treated with increasing disrespect by the owners at each meeting they attended. Following the latest rebuff they looked at each other and said, "That's it, let's go get a lawyer." The question will always linger whether taking the players' reps "into the family" would have made any difference in player-management relations in the long run or whether the big TV money wouldn't have strained the relationship eventually anyway.

By the end of the fifties the Players Association had achieved all kinds of gains, going far beyond the demands for heaters in the dugouts on cold nights, more towels, better meal money. Furthermore, they were setting the stage for the tremendous victories of the seventies, like the junking of the reserve clause, the elevation in status of the veteran, and financial benefits like collecting a salary for the whole season because you made it through till opening day.

At the end of the fifties the vacuum created in New York caused by the departure of the Dodgers and Giants screamed for corrective measures. The lead was taken by William Shea, a fast-moving far-ranging corporate lawyer who assembled a task force to bring another National League team back to New York. Shea's confreres included names like Barney Gimbel, department store tycoon and one-time father-in-law of Hank Greenberg; ex-Postmaster General Jim Farley, an old semi-pro first baseman; and the then-mayor of New York, Bob Wagner, who was a master of making New York operate seemingly like a Mercedes when actually there was just a little spit and twine holding the whole thing together. Then they got Branch Rickey, who had been in semi-retirement after having established the foundations for a Pittsburgh World Series victory in 1960.

From Olympus rumbled Rickey's pronouncement, "I am quite certain that within these United States there are sufficient first-class players to operate (in the) major league." Then, after a dramatic pause, "Inside or outside the present framework of baseball."

Around both leagues the telephones buzzed. "Jeez," was the reaction, "they're talking 'outlaw' league."

There hadn't been an "outlaw" league in baseball for more than forty years. The Federal League operated in 1914–15, and when it finally went under, a lot of money had been spent on both sides. One of the few legacies of that venture is Wrigley Field, built by the newcomers. And in the old record books you'll find names like George Stovall, Joe Tinker, Fielder Jones, and Bill McKechnie who managed in the Federal League.

This was no kids' stuff. There was ample money behind the newly named Continental League. It set up in New York, the media center of the country. Rickey, still a formidable figure at eighty, made news every time he spoke. And at every press conference Bill Shea, who usually presided, would begin things with . . . "God willing, as long as Mr. Rickey is with us. . . ."

Rickey lasted the life of the Continental and then some. The Continental had two wonderful years of proving a swift pain in the rear end to the vested interests who were reduced to holding secret war meetings and making plans to bolster the spots where the Continentals would provide a challenge.

The five original members of the Continental League were New York, Toronto, Houston, Denver, and Minneapolis. Later, Atlanta joined along with Ft. Worth-Dallas and Buffalo. That made it eight. It's interesting that all these cities, except Buffalo and Denver, now have major league baseball.

Not all were accepted into the charmed circle at the same time, but for starters the majors worked out a deal accepting two clubs immediately—New York and Houston.

Both went into the National League, breaking the eight-teams format. Both debuted in makeshift facilities pending the construction of new parks—New York in the old Polo Grounds, Houston's Colt 45's in a mosquito-infested playing field about a mile or two from the site of the Astrodome under construction. In the shuffling, Craig Cullinan, the young oil heir who had been out front in the Houston picture, disappeared and was replaced by Roy Hofheinz, a powerful politician who had been, among other things, Lyndon Johnson's campaign manager when Johnson ran for Congress.

The New York franchise became the Mets with Mrs. Joan Payson, former Giant red-hot, putting up most of the money. She was a Whitney and she and her brother John Hay (Jock) Whitney, owned the famed Greentree racing stable. Jock also owned the newspaper on which I worked most of my life, the *New York Herald Tribune*, having taken it over when the Reid family faltered. He blew an estimated $15 million before quitting and, though his other ventures absorbed the losses, it led him to wonder what would have happened had he taken that money and invested it in a radio station, or even a baseball club of his own.

Mrs. Payson turned the nuts and bolts of the operation over to her long time financial adviser-broker, Don Grant, but she retained a strong interest in the more exciting aspects of the game, like naming the club, for instance. First she announced, "Let's have a big contest for the best name," then she said, "let's have the sports writers name it, they know best." When we all got into the booze in her Fifth Avenue layout she said, "I want the club called the Larks because we're going to be playing in Flushing Meadow which makes me think of Meadowlarks. Not bad, eh boys?"

The boys had ideas of their own and hooted the suggestion into a corner. They came up with names like the " 'Liners" (for Skyline), "Burros" (for the five boroughs), and "Subways" (because everything in New York is linked via the subway system. But somehow the name Metropolitans, an early team in the National League, kept surfacing and one day everyone woke up and there were the New York Mets. And no prizes.

In their early days the Mets got a bit of kidding in heavily Germanic Cincinnati because there is a brand of German wurst known as "Metz." Casey Stengel out front, wryly waved it aside as just another example of regional loutishness.

No commitments had been made to the other clubs in the Continental League after the break-up. In Toronto, Jack Kent Cooke operated a while longer, then was attracted to pro basketball and the Lakers. In Denver, Bob Howsam became involved with the Denver Broncos in the American Football League, was bailed out by a job with the Cardinals, and later went on to head up a Cincinnati club which won a couple of World Series.

Minnesota got a franchise when the Senators quit Washington; Atlanta got theirs when Milwaukee carpet-bagged South, and the Dallas-Fort Worth area welcomed a second Washington deserter. So only Buffalo came up empty, and apparently will stay that way. When the eighty-thousand-seat suburban stadium was built in the early seventies, it was designed with football in mind.

Bill Shea had a stadium out by New York's busy LaGuardia

airport named after him. Everyone else either dropped out of sight or was absorbed by the establishment.

Branch Rickey died in the mid-sixties and his son, Branch, Jr., preceded him in death, but the family name carries on in baseball. Branch Rickey III, a grandson, is in the talent department of the Pirates.

12

The Cover Boys

IT IS NOT PARTICULARLY DIFFICULT to determine baseball's big box-office lures in the fifties. Riffle through the yellowing sports fan magazines and there they are—Mantle, Musial, Yogi, Campy, Ted Williams, Warren Spahn, Henry Aaron, Mays, Whitey Ford, Lew Burdette, Big Klu. Baseball was the big ticket in that sporting decade. The magazines, moving from twenty-five cents to fifty cents, followed the crowds and played it safely with resplendent color shots of the stars.

Once in a while a football player would shoulder in there, Unitas, Doak Walker, Alan Ameche, Jim Brown. Occasionally a roundball superstar like Bob Cousy or George Mikan would show up. But mostly it was baseball.

Ed Fitzgerald, now president of the Book of the Month Club, ran *Sport* Magazine when the Macfadden people owned it in the fifties, and he was a reasonably venturesome soul. He came up with the promotion idea of a complimentary sports car for the MVP in the World Series and later in the NFL championship game, since carried over to the Super Bowl. In his cover conferences Fitz looked at so many familiar faces he was starting to get a little punchy. Suddenly a super track star, the Olympic sprint ace, Bobby Joe Morrow from Texas, swam into his ken.

Bobby Joe had gone to Australia and brought back the Olympic gold medal. He had a sun-scorched crew cut, and he always appeared to be looking at the far-off mountain tops West of the Pecos. Fitz went with him on the cover defying the rule that at World Series time you have a ball player.

"We almost got killed," he recalled. "I never saw so many magazines returned."

Another yardstick is the yearly *Baseball Guide* published by the *Sporting News*. One year's cover invariably reflects the previous year's star or newsmaker. The breakdown of the ten covers covering the fifties is absorbing.

First, Casey Stengel is the only manager to appear. There was Casey on the '54 cover thanks to his having won five World Series in a row, an unparalleled feat.

After Casey come three outfielders, all Hall of Famers, Stan Musial, Mickey Mantle, and Ted Williams. Then three infielders, Red Schoendienst, being congratulated after a Cardinal homer, and the Yankee second-base–shortstop combination of Billy Martin and Jerry Coleman completing a double-play. One pitcher makes it, Robin Roberts, after his twenty-eight and seven season with the '52 Phillies.

Of three remaining covers one is an action shot, another is an ad for Spalding baseballs, and the last is the tattered Brooklyn Bum cartoon character, who is suddenly transformed into a garish movie-director type, admiring himself in the Hollywood mirror. This followed the Dodgers' first World Series victory in their new home.

The annual *Who's Who in Baseball*, that hip-pocket tome whose tiny type has put glasses on countless kid-fans, was another weather vane. There wasn't much creativity on the *Who's Who* covers, just the player the editors rated the best the previous year. They had a saver, the back cover that sometimes ran a house ad but usually offered a secondary figure.

Up front we find a total of five pitchers, Jim Konstanty, whose relief work pushed the Phillies into their first World Series in thirty-five years; Bobby Shantz, the franchise-saver (temporarily) with the Philadelphia Athletics; Hall of Famer Warren Spahn; Bob Turley; and Don Drysdale. The four outfielders are Stan the Man, Hank Sauer, who won MVP with the Cubs, Duke Snider, and Mickey Mantle. Infielders are Al Rosen and Alvin Dark.

A quick skimming will reveal one common denominator among the above. Everyone was white. No Roy Campanella, Jackie Robinson, or Willie Mays. As a sop the *Who's Who* used black players three times on the back cover, Campanella, Cleveland's hard-hitting second baseman, Bobby Avila (.341 in Cleveland's championship year), and the Dodgers' Don Newcombe.

These publications were distributed nationally and the rural South was, and still is, a big baseball market. The feeling was that a black player's picture on the cover wouldn't do much for newsstand sales.

But if Campy's feelings were hurt, how about Yogi Berra who was picked Most Valuable Player three times during the decade and never got a call? Admittedly no beauty winner, Yogi's face was as well known as any sports figure in the decade. If familiarity sells on the stands some publishing people made some profound mistakes.

By the fifties Yogi was an established star, feared throughout the American League as a "bad-ball" hitter. A "bad-ball" hitter can hit anything, even balls missing the strike zone.

The good "bad-ball" hitter, and there aren't many, simply slashes out and overpowers the poor pitch, sending it rocketing for extra bases or into the seats. A series of contortions may accompany this feat because sometimes he'll be swinging in the vicinity of his eyebrows.

Yogi had this ability until age diminished his skills in the early sixties. His batting average topped .300 only twice in the decade but he was the toughest of the Yankee outs and as a receiver he was virtually indestructible. When he suffered a busted nose during a road trip (a foul tip somehow came back right through the bars of his mask) they found some adhesive tape and patted it back to its approximate shape (with Yogi, one person's guess was as good as the next). After a day or two of chafing on the bench, Yogi was back there again doing knee-bends, or "push-ups" as he incorrectly described them.

Catching equipment, the mask, protector, and shin guards, has been known as "the tools of ignorance" for almost a century. The idea was that only someone with a low I.Q. would be silly enough to get back there behind the plate.

The Yogi Berra popularized by the media would seem to fit this pattern, a clown given to funny screw-ups of the English language. A lot of the lines the public read as attributed to Yogi, he was reading for the first time himself.

Although Yogi had the reputation of a clown, according to Dr. Sidney S. Gaynor, the Yankees' team physician, nothing could be further from the truth. "Yogi's no comedian," said the doctor. "He's a tense, nervous person and he worries a lot."

He was also lucky a lot, and he was the first to admit it. "I've been in the right place at the right time most of my life," said Yogi. But not always, like when he was at Omaha Beach on D-Day. The eighteen-year-old Berra, who was a very long way from the Dago Hill section of St. Louis where he grew up, was a rocket man on a thirty-six-foot landing craft en route to France without benefit of a passport.

Making money was never a problem for Yogi once he achieved the majors. He bought into a bowling alley with Phil Rizzuto over in New Jersey where both lived. They sold at a big profit just before bowling alleys became a dime a dozen, thanks to a national headlong program of over-building. About the same time he put a few bucks into a small chocolate drink company called Yoo-Hoo. It wasn't Coca-Cola but the investment multi-plied several hundredfold.

As a manager Yogi was the first in forty years to win

pennants in both leagues. With the Yankees he fought the Cardinals to seven games in the 1964 series and was bounced for his pains. With the Mets a decade later a disenchanted management procrastinated over firing him. Suddenly it became too late to do it. By the end of the season he had fooled everyone and had the Mets in the Series. That forced the club to keep him all of another season.

Yogi has had more books written about him than 98 percent of his peers. Exploring percentages it's probable that half the stories attributed to Yogi were apocryphal, but there is at least one I can vouch for 100 percent.

There was a day game in Chicago and Yogi went to the movies that evening. Several of us were sitting in the lobby when he returned.

"Where y'bin?" said someone.

"The movies," said Yogi. "Saw *Dr. Zhivago.*"

"How was it?" I said with genuine interest, not having seen the movie.

"Jeeze" said Yogi, "it was cold in Russia in them days."

You'll note all the preceding dialogue employs the word *said* instead of fancy words like *replied, answered, averred, insisted,* and all those other verbs which writers use to dress up conversation to keep the reader awake. That's because it was a pet peeve of Ernest Hemingway.

Hemingway always insisted that there was no better word than *said* in writing dialogue and please stop trying to improve on it.

Why drag in Hemingway? Man's been dead since 1961. Because Yogi met Hemingway in Toots Shor's saloon in New York one evening and they got kind of friendly around the bar. Toots, the proprietor who didn't blink an eye at presidents, industrial and union leaders, and famed scientists, was absolutely overwhelmed by the way these two pals of his had taken up with each other. He hovered behind them signaling frantically to Ziggy the bartender to keep their glasses filled.

Hemingway had to leave after a while to wrestle a lion or

shoot a water buffalo. After he was gone, Yogi said, "That Ernie's a pretty nice guy. Whatzee do?"

"He's a writer," said someone nearby.

"What paper?" said Yogi. That's what he said.

Roy Campanella, the other three-times MVP winner in the fifties, was the other super-catcher of the decade. Like Berra he was a superb handler of pitchers and awesome at the plate. His career was one of the great tragedies of the era, coming to an end in an auto accident which left him crippled.

It remains an open question whether or not the termination of Campanella's career had a direct effect on the Dodgers' fortunes. After successive World Series which they split with the Yankees, the Dodgers had dipped to third in 1957. Campy, who had shared the catching role with Rube Walker, hit a modest .242. The question will always linger whether this was only a slump in an up-and-down cycle (he hit .207 in 1954 between .300 seasons), or whether Campy's age was catching up with him.

He was listed as twenty-seven when he came to the Dodgers in 1948. But he had knocked around a long time in the Negro and Latin Leagues.

Roy came out of Philadelphia, the son of an Italian father and a Negro mother. The facade he offered was always a bright and merry one in contrast to Jackie Robinson's unyielding attitude once he had demonstrated his patently superior ability.

Robinson would frequently describe Campanella as an "Uncle Tom" because of his ability to get along with the establishment. There might have been just a trace of envy of Campy's ability to relate to all kinds of people.

After Campy's accident it turned out that the bright-and-merry was mostly window dressing. Like most, Campy had his problems, a difficult marriage being among them. And the difficulties were compounded in a wheelchair.

As a ball player, however, there was rarely any difficulty when he strode up there, took that long stance, and waved the bat menacingly.

In 1953, the year he hit his top total of forty-one homers, he had a three-homer afternoon in Cincinnati. Tired old Crosley Field slumbered in a low-rent district of Cincinnati, and there was a laundry across the street beyond left field. Three times Campanella came to bat with a man on first and Charley Dressen gave him the bunt sign. Each time Campy dutifully went through the motions of trying to lay one down, only to foul it up. Each time after that, he'd straighten up, take aim, and deposit the next pitch onto the roof of the laundry.

"The foul bunt," said one press box wag who had been witnessing this Dressen strategy all season. "Greatest play the Dodgers have. You foul it off a couple of times, then hit the next pitch out of the park. Wins a lot of ball games."

Campanella had a uniform on for the last time on September 29, 1957. If he had any doubts or misgivings about the season and the Dodgers' third-place finish behind the Braves he certainly didn't show them. He was busy with his large liquor business.

The Braves had taken the pennant on merit. Their biggest winner was Warren Spahn, twenty-one and eleven. The Dodgers' was Don Drysdale, seventeen and nine. Big Don Newcombe had dipped below .500 figures. Duke Snider was the Dodgers' big home-run hitter with forty, but Milwaukee's Hank Aaron had hit forty-four, the number emblazoned on the back of his shirt.

In Brooklyn the Boys of Summer were breaking up even as the baseball operation packed and dispatched its trucks westward to Los Angeles. Billy Cox, the third baseman, already was gone; the shortstop-second base combination of Charley Neal and Jim Gilliam had replaced PeeWee Reese and Jackie Robinson, with PeeWee moving to third. Change was in the air.

Pitchers like Sandy Koufax and Sal Maglie were five and four, six and six. Altogether it wasn't too much of a year for the Dodgers. But they survived it and went on to win championships and set attendance records in Los Angeles, which could scarcely contain its enthusiasm about its newly won major-league status.

Campy stayed behind, permanently chained to a wheelchair, a

paraplegic because of a neck injury suffered in that accident. He isn't the only one who has wondered, more than once, about the course of the Dodgers' history with him, as compared to without him. And had the rented car he drove that night responded on the icy turn the way his own car would have, it's most probable Campanella would have been the majors' first black manager, long before Frank Robinson was singled out for that distinction with Cleveland in 1975.

The cover boys in the outfield—Williams, Musial, Mays and Mantle (to list them in the order of their aggregate batting averages during this particular decade) sold a lot of tickets and generated a tremendous amount of interest. Williams, by design or otherwise, was the most controversial. He managed to fuel and maintain a running battle with the Boston press through a couple of generations, no mean feat. Frequently he'd be knocking some writer of the past the current group had never heard of. He remembered a lot besides the pitches certain moundsmen threw or the dimensions of the strike zone—dimensions, incidentally to which most of the umpires deferred.

Now Williams can derive whatever satisfaction he may wish from the fact that technological innovation, and public laziness has reduced the number of metropolitan papers in Boston from the original eight when he first showed up to two. When Williams went out of baseball he took most of his critics and sycophants with him, all unwilling fellow-travelers to the outer darkness where there is no paper-and-ink to carry one's daily outpouring of genius.

Williams' running fight with most of the news media is about as pertinent today as the question of whether the United States' refusal to join the League of Nations after World War I didn't wreck the prospects for world peace? His attitude was that he was entitled to his privacy which included a magisterial disregard for what he deemed stupid questions. The steerage conditions of the Boston press didn't make the situation easier.

The custom of assigning two men from each paper to cover a club made competition between reporters fierce. With it went a lot of sneaking around behind posts, examining of clubhouse trash, and loss of sleep worrying about whether the other guy on your own paper would be wiping you out the next day. To Williams' regularly vented scorn they retorted that his salary, which was an immense one, could be traced directly to public support of the ball club. Further, they represented the public.

Williams' average was .331 for the eight years he played in the fifties. He was gone for the '52-'53 season, called back for active duty as a Marine fighter pilot in the Korean War. The military, like baseball, agreed that Williams owned one of the better pairs of eyes in the entire United States. He eventually went on to a lifetime .344, finishing his baseball career as a manager.

Williams' role as a manager was slightly different from most. He needed neither money nor the acclaim. People in Washington convinced him that he owed it to the game which had given him so much. To return it Williams put in a dreary hitch in Washington and a few seasons in Texas after the franchise had been moved there.

Stan Musial also served baseball after his playing days but in a front-office capacity. Here too there was no need for salary. He had become an important figure in the hotel and restaurant business.

Musial came back as a senior vice-president of the Cardinals, the only organization he ever played for, either in the minors or during his twenty-two years in the big leagues, because he had been asked. Turning down the Cards would have been tantamount to turning down a member of the Musial family.

In the ten full years he performed in the fifties Musial hit at a .327 clip. Depending on your attitude, it was an easy .327 or a difficult one. The Cards finished half that time in the second division; they were never a winner. So it could be said there wasn't a great deal of pressure on him.

Conversely there is always the challenge of a superior craftsman trying desperately to improve the product. Easy or difficult he led the league in batting three times in the decade, the finest segment of his long career.

At the plate Stan Musial was something to see. When he came out of that batting crouch he resembled some giant spring uncoiling. Stainless steel, of course. At the end, a record of a .331 batting average and 475 homers guaranteed a quick ticket to the Hall of Fame.

Musial's more than two decades followed a modest $50 a month start as a pitcher in the West Virginia hills (Mountain States League). Only those who attended World Series games in the early part of the forties were privileged to see him perform in the post-season classic. In his second year he was the fourth-place hitter with the '42 Cards who beat the Yankees. He moved up to third in the batting order with the '43 club which lost to the Yankees, and had a .304 series against the Browns in the St. Louis intra-city Series the following year.

In 1946 Musial returned from the Navy and played in what was his final Series, a seven-game effort under Eddie Dyer, with St. Louis beating the Red Sox.

Much has been made of the fact that Musial would never have had a career if it hadn't been for the persistence of Dickie Kerr, one-time White Sox pitcher who had Musial in the minors when his pitching arm went dead. Sensing something special in Musial's hitting, Kerr prevailed on him to stick with it. He further befriended the Musials during the arrival of their first child.

Said Musial about his early years: "I was a kid who didn't want to fail in front of my friends, so when I signed with the Cardinals I asked them to send me to a club not too close to home." Not-too-close was Williamson, West Virginia.

On the 240-mile bus trip Musial's doubts burgeoned. If the general manager of the club hadn't met him at the bus station late at night he'd have turned right around and gone back to Donora, Pennsylvania.

"It was tough making it on fifty dollars a month," he recalled, "and my mother used to send me a five-dollar bill in the mail every week."

"They could tell from my letters when I was getting homesick and they'd come down on the bus on Sunday and bring me a home-cooked meal."

Meals from back in Donora, lugged in a basket; five dollars of his father's sweat in the mail! No wonder Musial murdered National League pitching through four Presidential administrations.

Willie Mays played only seven seasons in the fifties. He came up in '51, the same year as Mickey Mantle, and the Army grabbed him for two years. When he returned he hit at a brisk .345 in the year in which the Giants not only won the pennant but swept the Series with the Indians.

Mays hit .347 that first year in San Francisco and was more than a little disappointed when the locals adopted Orlando Cepeda, the Puerto Rican Baby Bull who had never played in New York, as their hero. There are those who would say that those West Coast sophisticates (For goodness sakes, the ladies showed up wearing hats and gloves at the ball games.) wanted nothing that smacked of New York. Cepeda was mint-fresh material.

Mays was Leo Durocher's boy all the way. "Mr. Leo," Willie would call to him shrilly in a mock yell for help. With his clothes off Mays was probably the most impressive of the four superstars we've been speaking about. He was no professor of economics and he'd come up a little short discussing the Malthusian theory, but he was paid, and paid well, not for conversation but for hitting the ball when the Giants were up and going and getting it when the other team was at bat. And not too many could stay close to him in either department.

Mays had another edge going for him. He worked for an owner, Horace Stoneham, who was a fan. There were precious few things Willie wanted that went ungratified as long as Horace was able to pick up a phone or write a check.

Almost as many books—some of which he actually read—have been written by and about Willie Mays as about any of the game's stars. One of the stories of his earlier life-and-times is worth re-telling, and it came after the Giants had moved to San Francisco.

One of the writers covering the ball club was Charley Einstein of the *San Francisco Examiner*. Einstein spun off into book-writing and Mays was a logical choice and a quick sale. Mays agreed, and over the season Charley would sit down and pick Willie's brains on various aspects of his career and the game.

With the season ended, Charley collected all his notes in the pleasant California autumn and sat down at the typewriter but some items needed clarification. He had Willie's unlisted number.

"Hello Willie? This is Charley."

A large silence from the other end, although it was obvious the phone was in Mays' hand. Finally, "Charley who?"

"Charley Einstein."

Again a large silence, although Einstein could hear breathing.

A little desperately, "You know, Charley Einstein, the fellow who is doing the book with you."

Willie: "What book?"

Mickey Mantle's .309 represents nine seasons of the fifties. He ranged from .267 his first year, when he split the season between New York and Kansas City, to .365 in 1957. His best year with the wagon-tongue was 1956 when he won the Triple Crown with a batting average of .353, 52 homers, 130 RBIs. Few will contest that he was the leading switch hitter of all time.

Of this group of cover boys Mickey was the only one who played in the first World Series game he ever saw. He was in right field, leading off for the Yankees against the Giants in 1951. Joe DiMaggio, finishing up was in center, Hank Bauer in left. Mickey wasn't twenty.

Mickey went on to eleven more World Series in which he racked up all kinds of records, such as the following, all enduring marks: home runs (18), runs scored (42), runs batted in (40), total bases (123), most long hits (26), most extra bases on long hits (64), most walks (43), most strikeouts (54), most Series played by an outfielder (12), most games played by an outfielder (63).

Of this quartet of superstars Mantle represents the greatest triumph of mind over body. He was an osteomyelitis victim as a high-schooler, the result of a kick on the shin sustained playing football in Commerce, Oklahoma. It kept him out of the Army during the Korean War and it also bothered him more than a little during a decade and a half in baseball. He was a slow healer as a result of the original infection and it took twice as long for him to recover from his several knee operations as the normal person.

Even so, he was the biggest draw of the decade; but luck played an all-important role in his success story, going back to the time Yankee scout Tom Greenwade discovered him in the Ozarks and offered him a bonus of $1,150. Greenwade based the bonus on what Mickey might lose by giving up working in the zinc mines around Spavinaw with his father and playing semi-pro ball, also with his father. From this figure was subtracted the sixty dollars monthly salary with the Independence club in the KOM (Kansas-Oklahoma-Missouri) League.

Mantle ultimately went on to enjoy national acclaim, a person for whom presidents made room, but in the winter of '50–'51 he was just another name being pushed by the Yankees' publicity man as a possible comer who could replace DiMaggio. Mantle had hit .383 in Class C ball at Joplin, Missouri in 1950 as a shortstop. But he had to be doing something incorrectly in the field because he had fifty-five errors.

As a conductor of a hot-stove column in the *New York Herald Tribune* I dropped him a routine note asking for a few pertinent facts which might possibly bring a hint of spring to the winter-morning breakfast table. The kid replied promptly in a note on dime-store pad paper. He printed the note in the fashion then popular in educational circles.

It was a friendly enough note. In it he said that Phil Rizzuto was his idol, that he had committed seventy errors as shortstop (He even made an error adding up his errors.), and he mentioned that business about the kick in the leg. Also, there were two brothers who would be even better than he, Roy and Ray. They were to get no further than A ball in the Yankee organization.

Years later the note was mentioned to Mantle after it found its way into the Jim Thorpe Oklahoma Sports Hall of Fame. He didn't remember it, but he remembered his figures, and that he'd have hit .400 that year except he simply couldn't get a hit in his last two weeks. Moreover, he started to get upset just remembering his early travail. Then he shrugged it off. "But it's funny, I don't remember ever writing that letter," mused Mickey. "I didn't think I could write in those days."

"You didn't," was the reply. "You printed it."

13

Baseball's Greatest Hits

DURING THE SUMMER OF '76 when the country was celebrating its two hundredth birthday, baseball coincidentally celebrated its hundredth anniversary.

The National League had been founded one wintry evening in February, 1876 in a hotel on what is now New York's lower Broadway. It was a matter of such gravity that no newspaper gave an account of the proceedings until four days later. It was a secret almost as well-kept as that of Abner Doubleday's inventing the game thirty-seven years earlier.

Communications and public relations were to become a lot better a century later. The game's horn-blowers came up with what they said were the results of a national poll detailing (1), Baseball's all-time most memorable moments and (2), Baseball's all-time great personalities. They squeezed a lot of mileage out of these listings and a bit more will be forthcoming because they're listed again here even though the balloting was probably as authentic as a three-dollar bill. How can you resist recalling:

1. Hank Aaron's 715th home run?
2. Bobby Thomson's "home run heard 'round the world?"
3. Don Larsen's perfect-game pitching in the 1956 World Series?
4. Babe Ruth's "called shot" which, according to his manager, Joe McCarthy, he never made?
5. Joe DiMaggio's fifty-six-game hitting streak in 1941?

Or consider the following most memorable baseball personalities:

1. Babe Ruth
2. Casey Stengel
3. Dizzy Dean
4. Willie Mays
5. Ted Williams
6. Tie, Mickey Mantle and Hank Aaron
8. Roberto Clemente
9. Ty Cobb
10. Jackie Robinson

A bit of analysis performed on both lists brings ample rewards. First the "moments." Two of the five, or forty percent, occurred during the fifties, again underlining the importance of this particular decade to the game.

Then, take the personalities. By whatever yardstick is employed, the fifties proved highly productive in this category, too. Of the top ten, seven either emerged from, or played in some segment of the fifties. These were Casey Stengel, Willie Mays, Ted Williams, Mickey Mantle, Hank Aaron, Roberto Clemente, and Jackie Robinson

Just what constitutes a "personality" is something tucked away deep in the cerebellum of those balloting, real or fancied. Just as Judy Crist, the movie critic, once observed, "One man's perversion is another man's hobby," so one man's personality choice could easily prove another's great big yawn. F'rinstance, no one polled me but how could you leave out Pepper Martin or Pete Gray?

Pepper played for the St. Louis Gashouse Gang in the thirties. Known as the Wild Horse of the Osage, Martin came out of the dust-bowl country and played as though he was fearful he'd be sent back to suffocate in the clouds of airborne alfalfa fields if he didn't put out 135 percent on every play. Where he came from, underwear and appurtenances like jock straps would have been laughed right off the general-store counter. So he played with nothing between him and the terrain at Sportsman's Park, but his Cardinals uniform. Strong men cringed when Pepper Martin slid into second base on his belly.

Or Pete Gray, a St. Louis performer of a later era who played one season with the Browns and hit .218 as an outfielder? You think I'm a little nuts talking about a .218 hitting outfielder? This one had one arm.

You saw him in action catching the ball with his glove, flipping the ball into the air while whipping his glove under the armpit of his missing arm, catching the descending ball and pegging into the infield and you never quite forgot it.

Or how about Billy Cox, the Dodgers third baseman who used to field a blazing hopper and then, almost in slow motion, used to turn the ball so that he could finally read the signature of Warren Giles, president of the National League. He'd check the spelling, and then he'd fire it over to Gil Hodges with blinding speed for the close call at the bag. Or on another level how about the Yankee outfielder who claimed to have been a journalism major at a Big Ten school and sought to prove it by picking up two doses of gonorrhea in a single season? It tied the major league record, shared by several.

Most of the names listed in the personality group, with the exception of Roberto Clemente, are treated at some length in other segments of this narrative. Clemente, originally a Dodger farmhand, was grabbed off by Pittsburgh for something like eight thousand dollars in the draft because Brooklyn was unable to protect his status in their minor-league system due to a bonus arrangement. Branch Rickey, the Pittsburgh president, was fairly familiar with that bonus arrangement. When he was with Brooklyn he had okayed it.

When the Dodgers fired Rickey and he went to Pittsburgh to build yet another pennant winner his first priority move was to draft Clemente, who warmed up through the latter half of the fifties to become a superstar of the sixties. He met a tragic end in the seventies, dying in a plane crash while en route from his native Puerto Rico with medical and rescue supplies for earthquake victims in Central America.

The plane, a charter, never got more than a few miles offshore before it crashed. The mandatory five-year waiting period for inclusion in the Hall of Fame was waived and Clemente became a member the following year.

Clemente was a complainer. He complained that he played with aches and pains which would have sidelined most others. He complained that the news media had called him Bob, going along with the name the club printed on the roster, rather than by his correct name, Roberto. And one night I listened to him berate in labored English the New York chapter of the Baseball Writers Association at its annual dinner. The reason Clemente had the mike was that the writers were honoring him as Player-of-the-year and there were a lot of surprised scribes in the hall as Clemente burned their ears. His beef was, "Why now, when he had been just as good ten years earlier?"

In the memorable moments department, Joe DiMaggio's 56-game streak in 1941, starting May 15 and ending July 17, can scarcely qualify as a "moment." Rather it was a series of them. The others, though, can be frozen like a frame in a TV instant replay—Aaron's home run shot in the Atlanta ballpark; Thomson's liner into the lower deck of the Polo Grounds which won the 1951 National League playoff; and the half-swing by Dodgers' Dale Mitchell at a strike in the '56 Series which ended Don Larsen's perfect game at Yankee Stadium; and Babe Ruth's so-called "called shot" in the '32 Series against the Cubs in Wrigley Field. That's where the Babe, a little irritated by the jockeying from the Cub bench after taking a couple of strikes, allegedly pointed where he was going to put the next pitch, then did.

Forty years later, shortly before he died, Hall of Fame manager Joe McCarthy, Ruth's field leader that afternoon, was taping some recollections with Don Honig, one of the leading oral historians of the game. McCarthy was in a position to tell the whole truth. He had been there and he was at the age—well into his nineties—when it doesn't make much difference if you decided to tell the truth.

McCarthy retained his buttons right till the end. When Honig brought up the Ruth "pointing" incident McCarthy told him: "I won my first pennant with the Yankees in '32 and we played my old team in the Series that year, the Cubs. Beat them four straight. McCarthy won three World Series in four-game sweeps, 1932, 1938 (vs. Cubs again) and 1939 (vs. Reds). That's more World Series games than some of his managing contemporaries even attended.

"It wasn't a very friendly World Series. There were some pretty rough bench jockeys on both sides. The Cubs were on Ruth an awful lot. Babe had a knack for stirring things up, you know.

"A lot of people still believe today that he really did that (point to the bleachers, then sock one there). Did he? You see the Cubs were riding him from the bench every time he came to the plate and finally he pointed over at them. Then he hit the next pitch out. After he hit the ball somebody said, 'Did you see where he pointed?' Well, a lot of them did see his hand go up and they said, 'Maybe he did point that way.' That's how the story began. Tell you the truth I didn't see him point anywhere at all, but I might have turned my head for a moment.

"Babe went along with it. He was a great showman, you know. But later on he admitted that he never pointed to the bleachers. Gabby Hartnett said the same thing (Cubs catcher) and Charlie Root (Cubs pitcher) also said that. They said he pointed to the Cubs dugout."

A generation later two of the five "memorable moments" followed within five years of each other. Bobby Thomson's homer off Ralph Branca was walloped in 1951; Don Larsen pitched his perfect World Series game in 1956. For both it was a high point in a journeyman's career. Both could make a living in the game today but neither would get a call in the Hall of Fame balloting. Larsen actually lost more games than he won over his fourteen-year career, and never won more than eleven games in any single season. Yet he is a bigger attraction today at things like celebrity golf tournaments and business meetings than pitchers who have won twice that number.

Another oddity is that both these historic events took place in New York City. The old Polo Grounds, where a housing project now stands, was on the other side of the Harlem River across from Yankee Stadium. It was called the Polo Grounds because it was much too small to accommodate polo, and it was suited more for football than for baseball. It was shaped basically like a running track, long and thin.

The lines from home plate to the base of the twenty-foot concrete walls in both right and left field were supposed to measure 257 feet. Leonard Koppett, at that time a young newspaperman with lots of ideas, once stepped it off using the toe-heel-toe method. After about 240 of these steps he found his nose pressed against solid concrete.

Giant scouts were always looking for dead pull-hitters because you could drive one four hundred feet up the middle and if the fielder was fleet enough it was just a loud out. Thomson was a sound .270 hitter, but he was no pull artist. In other words, he couldn't be counted upon to come through with that particular kind of a hit in a particular situation.

Bobby Thomson was the principal actor in those four days which literally shook the 1951 baseball world but there were a flock of supporting performers, Leo Durocher, the Giants manager; Charlie Dressen, his Dodger counterpart; Ralph Branca, the pitcher; Clyde Sukeforth, the Dodger bullpen coach; Don Mueller, who fractured his ankle in the last game; Clem Labine, who pulled the Dodgers back into the contention with a great pitching job in the second game; the broadcasters, Russ Hodges and Red Barber; and Henry Thompson, who was spiked earlier in the season.

Although it is now mostly forgotten, Thompson was one of the first black men in the game. Whoever owned the Browns in 1947 decided to participate in breaking the color line with a couple of ball players from the Negro Leagues. It was probably a box-office move against the more powerful Cardinals, who were standing pat with their all-white hand. At the time Jackie Robinson was already in Brooklyn, Larry Doby was in Cleveland.

Thompson didn't last too long with the Browns. But he turned up again, this time in the Giants organization, and he stuck. He wasn't too big a fellow but he was purposeful. In his record section was an item glossed over. He had murdered a man down in Texas.

Details of how Henry beat the Lone Star life rap are hazy but those concerning his post-career capers in New York are still amusing. After his playing days he settled in New York and one night found himself a trifle short of cash. So he went to a place where he had spent a lot of it in his day, his corner whiskey store.

"What'll it be, Hank?" asked the proprietor cheerily.

"Nuthin' this time," announced Henry, "This is a stickup." And to underscore the point he pointed a gun at the storekeeper.

There is a certain element of danger in holding up people, especially those you know. The proprietor didn't bother trying to talk Henry out of his criminal ways. He reached way under the counter for a Louisville Slugger he kept for such contingencies and fetched Thompson a right smart blow, not enough to knock him out but sufficient to cause him to flee in pain and confusion.

Then the proprietor called the cops who were a little embarrassed when they went around to Henry's apartment to grab a fellow they used to cheer for at the Polo Grounds. He was such a nice guy.

Horace Stoneham, the Giants boss who still had a little

political clout left around town before he was forced to the West Coast, probably got Thompson off with nothing more severe than a rough tongue lashing. The judge probably told him to change his grog shops.

Henry Thompson was a Giant first-year man in '51 and rapidly won the third-base job. Then a spike wound took him out of the lineup.

That gave Bobby Thomson, without the "p," another chance. Bobby was essentially an outfielder but he was having a little trouble breaking into a starting group that now included Willie Mays, Monte Irvin, and Don Mueller.

Over in Brooklyn, Charlie Dressen had replaced Branch Rickey's man, Burt Shotton, as field boss. It appeared a sound pick. Early in July the Dodgers won eight straight for a nine-and-one-half-games lead over the second-place Giants. Said Dressen, never one to hold back when he saw pencils poised, "We knocked them out; they'll never bother us again."

On July 20 the Dodgers started still another winning streak, ten straight and seventeen out of twenty through the first half of an August 11 doubleheader. That made their lead thirteen and one-half games. (They lost the second game so the next day their lead was a mere thirteen.) That date also had additional historical significance. The first game of that twin bill with the Boston Braves marked the first baseball color telecast.

Just as you mark a child's height on the wall, this would have been a good place for Charlie Dressen to have made that pencil mark. The Giants started on a streak of their own the following day. Sixteen in a row, all but three registered at home. When it was over, the Dodgers lead had dwindled to five games.

There it stayed a while. At the start of the final western trip for both clubs the Dodgers were five and a half in front. They managed to slice only one game from that figure during the trip. When both teams returned it appeared to be all over.

But things started to bubble. The Dodgers lost two out of three to the Phillies and the Giants beat the Braves three in a row. Now it was only two and a half. Then it became only one, when the Giants won at Philly and the Dodgers lost a doubleheader to the Braves.

Toward the end of that final week the Giants had a couple of open dates and the Dodgers were busy losing a couple. First they finished up a series in Boston losing on a disputed call. The umpire at home plate ruled someone slid under Campanella, always bad, but with the winning run as well. Campy argued that one hotly, his teammates joined, and the arbiters cleared the Dodger bench.

Still bitter and argumentative, the Dodgers carried their dispute off the field, took turns kicking the door of the umpire dressing room which remained discreetly shut although there wasn't any doubt on the other side of the door about the obscenities being hurled at it. The kicks splintered a couple of lower panels. The umpires reported these shenanigans, and Campanella and Jackie Robinson were each fined one hundred dollars. Preacher Roe, the skinny lefthander, was nailed for a more modest fifty dollars. The fellow who had done most of the kicking and screaming got off scot-free. Baseball hasn't changed much.

Then the Dodgers went down to Philly and blew a three-run lead and there it was; a first-place tie with two days to go.

In Boston, on a Saturday afternoon Sal Maglie shut out the Braves for the Giants. Down in Philadelphia, the Dodgers' Don Newcombe matched it. Still tied. Now it was down to that last day.

Larry Jansen went out to wrap it up for the Giants. No problem here. He pitched a five-hitter, won 3–2. The Giants played that game in tired old Braves Field with split vision, one eye on the opposition, the other on the scoreboard. And with reason.

Down in Philadelphia the Dodgers were having all sorts of trouble. The Phillies jumped on Preacher Roe and led 6–1 after three innings. Two innings later they were still up front, 8–5.

Up in Boston the Giants were dressing in a hurry to make that five o'clock good train that got you into New York at a reasonably civilized hour. They always shot for the five o'clock. It even had a better diner than the others.

They made this one by a close margin. The conductor had held the train for about ten minutes or so because the Giants were traditionally good tippers. Now they'd get the rest of the Dodger game on radio, or at least they'd be getting scores. Someone would have a portable radio. You couldn't hear too good with one of these on the train, pre-transistors, but if you sort of held it against the window, it made things a little better. They even came equipped with a suction cup for this purpose.

But wouldn't you know; when they settled down and Durocher barked "Turn on the damn radio and let's see how badly they beat those bastards," there wasn't a single radio aboard.

Leo cursed a little, then said, "Well, we'll make a call at the next stop." He grabbed the Pullman conductor's sleeve as he was passing through the diner where the Giants were assaulting two-inch steaks. "Hey, Colonel," brayed Leo, "How much time will we have in Providence? Enough to make a phone call?"

"Maybe about four or five minutes, that's all," he advised. "We're running about five minutes late because we held for you up in Boston."

A few additional obscenities from Leo. Nothing to do now but sit and look out at the scenery. Never mind what was happening around Kingston, Rhode Island, what was doing down in Philly? Had the Dodgers gotten their just desserts or did them sum-'bitches pull another one out? A few desultory gin games were started on the stained tablecloths; others thumbed through the Sunday sports sections with their day-old box scores long since memorized back at breakfast. The one score they were really interested in was locked in the ozone somewhere.

Now they were finally in New Haven. A fifteen-minute stop. "Arch," snapped Durocher at a newsman who rated Leo one notch above John Peter Zenger, "Get your ass to a phone and call one of your newspaper friends and find out what happened to the Dodgers."

Arch was back in a few minutes. The players, jammed into the vestibule, didn't have to be told. Everything sagged on old Arch, his crew-cut, his suspenders, the baggy pants held up in haphazard fashion, his Ivy League socks.

"They won it in the fourteenth," he declared.

This time Leo didn't curse. No time for that sort of luxury. His features merely sharpened and he announced, "All right everybody, we're working tomorrow. It'll be Hearn pitching for us." The latter announcement was for the benefit of the newsmen to whom Leo's pitching choice would be important.

Down in Philadelphia just about everybody on the club was pitching for the Dodgers. After the spitballing Roe had been eliminated Dressen came on with Ralph Branca, Clyde King, Clem Labine, Carl Erskine, Newcombe, and Bud Podbeilan. Podbeilan pulled it out after Newcombe had walked a couple with two out in the thirteenth.

A whole new generation of baseball fans has come to maturity without ever having seen Connie Mack Stadium, formerly the home of two Philadelphia teams. It was small by today's standards, squarish rather than the utilitarian oval, which accommodates baseball and football and soccer in today's ball parks.

The press box in that rat's nest was one of the highest lookouts in the majors. All you could see from it were a lot of tops of baseball caps. Additionally, the lighting was substandard. Energy saving was fashionable in Philly twenty-five years before its time.

The newsmen covering this final epic were a little punchy by now. Squeezed by approaching deadlines they had been juggling leads in their heads since the ninth inning, i.e., "Giants-Yankees in World Series," "Giants-Dodgers in playoff," "extra innings." Also there was the Sunday law prohibiting the turning on of those lousy lights, anyway. They'd finish by the light of a pack of matches lit by the umpire around home plate, if necessary.

The accounts of that day, including my own, had Robinson saving the game with a diving catch on Eddie Waitkus' liner in the twelfth, then winning it with a homer in the fourteenth. My description more than hinted that Robinson had scooped the ball on a skidding bounce, and when he saw he had no chance for a play at the plate, he faked the umpires out of their shoes with a dramatic fall, rising ever so slowly to his feet, holding the ball a moment before rolling it to the pitcher's mound.

If anyone had any doubts about the authenticity of the play, it was obvious that Robinson, from his actions, had not. And that's the way it went down in the books—Waitkus lined to Robinson for the third out. Neither are around anymore to bear testimony either way, and anyway, ball players tend to stick with what's in the record.

The Dodgers had won the game and the next battle was the mile walk to the North Philadelphia train station. They had a lot of people riding shotgun for them, fending off the natives who didn't believe Robinson had caught that liner, either. A lot of people had come down from Brooklyn to root for their favorites, unable to believe that a team that had a thirteen-game lead in mid-season was going to lose it all on the last day.

They didn't, and at eleven the next morning they reported to Ebbets Field for the first of a three-game playoff with the Giants. There is no record of how much sleep the principals got but one Dodger who slept with his clothes on was Walter O'Malley, their boss. He stayed up most of the night negotiating and arranging a CBS transcontinental live telecast of the game since he owned the rights.

A year earlier it wouldn't have been necessary for him to bother. The lack of facilities would have made it impossible. What brought it within reach was the opening earlier in the year of AT&T's first micro-wave relay system.

The ticket people didn't take off their clothes, either. Today, tickets are printed by computer with all those funny-looking numbers, but then it was a painstaking hand job, with constant checking and re-checking. Then there were the concessions people who had put their pots and pans and labor-availability lists away for the season. Ushers had to be rounded up. And the cops had to provide one of those sizeable emergency details.

The historic day was warm and hazy, a beautiful Indian summer day which put a pleasing patina on New York. When the players arrived the crowd had already begun streaming through the bleacher gates. They had been lining up all night behind one particular nut camped there for a week wanting to be the first customer for what he thought would be the World Series between Brooklyn and the New York Yankees. Through the long, dark hours of that final night he had held his ground trading abuse with Giant fans around him. Finally, when the gates opened he drew a deep breath and shouted, "To hell with this. I'm not going in there. I hate the Giants."

Inside, Leo Durocher was also falling back on the "to Hell with it" routine. Sports media people from all over the North American continent were bombarding him with questions and Leo was shooting answers right back. Leo was in the baseball business for almost a half-century and there is no record of his ever saying, "No comment," or "That's off the record."

Leo, how does it feel to be a miracle worker?

"To hell with that," advised Durocher, "It's a brand new season now, isn't it? It's a new game. For cash money."

Here was a Durocher at his absolute best. In a tight corner, all right, but then so was the other son of a bitch, too, wasn't he?

There was one thing rivals learned about Durocher early, in addition to his feeling more comfortable than most in a tight spot. He permitted you to make no mistakes. If you did, bang, you were gone. It was a Durocher who might not signal for a duster at his grandmother's graying head but he'd most certainly brush her back just a little from that plate. That was the Durocher who ran things throughout the first game.

He was almost hysterical with glee when Bobby Thomson blasted a two-run homer off Ralph Branca, the Dodgers' opening pitcher. In the eighth, Monte Irvin sent one into the lower left field deck. That was the three to one ball game.

There was a significant development in that opening game. Roy Campanella, slated to win the first of his three Most Valuable Player awards, didn't get the ball out of the infield.

The day before, sliding in that final fourteenth inning in Philadelphia, he had pulled a thigh muscle.

Campy fought off suggestions he take himself out of the lineup but he wasn't much use in it. He bounced out three times, once on a double play ball that stifled a big Brooklyn threat in the fourth inning. The next day, up at the Polo Grounds, Doc Wendler, the Dodgers' trainer, sprayed it with numbing methyl chloride, but it didn't work. The slow-footed Rube Walker caught the rest of the way.

Walker didn't do badly in the playoffs. He got four hits in nine trips including a homer in the ten to nothing rout the following day. Clem Labine baffled the Giants before and after a forty-minute rain delay in the sixth. He had toured the dugout lifting turned-down corners on people's mouths with "Cheer up, it isn't over yet." And he was right. In comparison to the sell-out at Ebbets Field, only thirty-eight thousand watched this one. There were fifteen thousand empties.

There were an additional four thousand unoccupied pews for the big one the next day with all that "cash money," Leo's favorite expression, on the line. In years to come the people who were to claim they had seen the homer would run about a million. The turnstiles told a different story.

October 3 was another overcast day. They had to switch on the lights by the third inning. Considering the stakes, it was a fast game, taking less than two and one-half hours.

There had been some talk that Preacher Roe, the lefthander, would be Dressen's starting choice. But Preach' couldn't come up for this one. His skinny frame had taken one beating too many in the last two weeks. It had to be Newcombe or nothing.

Durocher, of course, met trump with trump. And a little better. Maglie would start; Larry Jansen would relieve, if necessary. Both were twenty-three-game winners.

Maglie was good, Newk was even better. The Dodgers had a 1-0 lead until the Giants tied it in the seventh. Then the Barber was pounded for three runs in the eighth on four hits, a wild pitch that permitted PeeWee Reese to score, and an intentional pass to Jackie Robinson. Now that was a little more like the Dodgers of late July and early August. See you at the Yankee-Dodgers World Series, pal.

The impression that nothing was going to change grew stronger when Henry Thompson rolled out as a pinch-hitter for Maglie in the eighth. In the ninth Jansen came in, got the Dodgers three in a row. Now it was just three Giant outs to the World Series. The Dodgers never got them.

Alvin Dark opened with a fifth Giant hit off Newcombe. For some reason Gil Hodges decided to play close to first base obviously trying to hold Dark from taking too big a lead. Whatever dictated this questionable strategy, it backfired and Don Mueller, a bat manipulator almost as deft as Dark, slapped one through the hole where Hodges should have been playing.

Dark scampered all the way to third on that one. Irvin stepped to the plate, representing the tying run. He lifted a pop foul to Hodges, Gil wasn't out of position on that one. One out.

Newcombe lifted his cap and mopped his brow with the back of his pitching hand. Then he stretched and threw to the plate where Whitey Lockman connected with a sharp crack. Two bases into left. One run.

Mueller injured his ankle sliding into third and was replaced by Clint Hartung. Ralph Branca and Carl Erskine had been warming up far out in the left field bullpen. Dressen had been on the phone from the inning's start with Clyde Sukeforth, the bullpen catcher. "Who's got better stuff?" he demanded. "Branca," said Sukey.

Now Branca was plodding in, taking his time—and there was lots of it available—to mull over the consequences of a possible bad pitch. Branca was a big, shy, intelligent fellow coming out of New York University to pitch for the Dodgers, and had been a twenty-game winner. He had once endeared himself to Durocher-haters by insulting Leo's wife, actress Laraine Day. She had made a derogatory remark about the Dodgers after Leo had left the club for the Giants. Branca countered with "What the hell is she talking about? She doesn't know the difference between a baseball and an onion." It's an observation that has resisted the erosion of the years.

Onre in the vicinity of the mound Branca studiously avoided Dressen's darting glances, scarcely hearing the change-of-guard litany between manager and reliever with the counterpoint from the catcher. This had been going on for more than a week, anyway. All old stuff. Don't give him anything good but strike the sum'bitch out. Yeah.

Branca nodded. He felt the automatic slap on the seat of his pants, that parting gesture to indicate confidence. Now it was him against Bobby Thomson who had already connected for two hits and a scoring fly.

Thomson was in a peculiar position awaiting that first pitch. Sure, he had been hitting. He had also over-run first base in the inning he singled. Scrambling back when he realized second base was slightly occupied, he had been thrown out easily. If the Giants blew it that boo-boo could stick in their minds a long time.

Thomson recalled his wait during the pitching change as one of odd detachment. He watched the groundskeepers with interest, as they were carrying Mueller across the field toward the clubhouse beyond centerfield. They moved at an unhurried gait.

"I was nervous and tense in the dugout," he recalled later. "I could feel it in my arms and legs but once I got up there with the bat it all disappeared."

Branca's first pitch to Thomson caught the outside corner for a strike. It was high, though, and Thomson blinked a little. High stuff was his meat and potatoes. Had Ralph forgotten?

Branca got Rube Walker's return toss and stared hypnotically past Thomson, deeply crouched. He shot a final look at Hartung, pinch-running at third, then fired.

The next voice you will hear will be that of the late Russ Hodges, Giants broadcaster, exactly as it was recorded off the radio by a local fan. Hodges' radio station, with a remarkable non-sense of history, hadn't bothered. We pick him up with the count at one strike.

"Bobby's hitting at two-ninety-two. He's had a single and a double and he drove in the Giants' first run with a long fly to center. Brooklyn leads four-two. Hartung down the line at third, not taking any chances. Lockman, without too big a lead at second, but he will be running like the wind if Thomson hits one. Branca throws.

"There's a long fly . . . it's gonna be . . . I believe . . . the Giants win the pennant. The Giants win the pennant. The Giants win the pennant. The Giants win the pennant.

"Bobby hit into the lower deck of the left field stands. The Giants win the pennant and they're going crazy, they're going crazy. I don't believe it. I don't believe it. I don't believe it. I will NOT believe it.

"Bobby Thomson hit a line drive into the lower deck of the left field stands and the place is going crazy. The Giants, Horace Stoneham's got a winner. The Giants win it by a score of five to four. And they're picking up Bobby Thomson and carrying him off the field."

That was it, except for a few excursions of fancy. Twenty-five years later someone who hadn't been there among the million who were supposed to have seen the shot, stretched it all into a book. Writing about things you haven't seen inevitably presents slight obstacles, like having to take people's words on things you might ordinarily question. Sometimes you hear strange items, like the story that during the hysteria and confusion generated by the occasion, a couple of young enthusiasts, hopefully at least acquainted, figured some sexual intercourse would be fitting and appropriate for the no-longer sacred turf of the Polo Grounds. Maybe.

I can't definitely cancel this bit of Americana since I was in no position to see what was happening, even though I was very much among the "million" in the ball park that afternoon. I can definitely state though, that in the note-exchanging among a dozen reporters in frantic post-mortems, it didn't come up. Had it happened the chances are pretty good that one of us would have spotted it.

My vantage point wasn't the best. I was in the Dodger clubhouse awaiting the victors and the pearls scheduled to drop from their lips. On big games you always had several men, someone to do the over-all story, another for individual locker room stories, and the third for general notes.

So there I was, listening to it all on the radio from the eighth inning on. The only view of the field was through a narrow window, the kind our forebears used to aim through hoping to nail an Indian or two. This one was blocked completely by the 350-pound proportions of Happy Felton, an elephantine announcer who did the Dodgers' pre- and post-game shows known as *Talk to the Stars.* He too was awaiting the return of the Dodgers to put his star pick on the air. He was also a close friend and hunting companion of Walter O'Malley.

There was this roar which carried clear through the walls and I made a reflex rush toward the blocked window just as Happy Felton was rushing away from it.

"What happened?" I shouted.

Felton's answer was a harried, "Lemme out of here. I gotta get out of here." He had seen the ball dropping into the left field seats. He had no desire to be around when O'Malley came into the dressing room.

There's a famous photo which still pops up occasionally showing Branca slumped on the steps inside the dressing room, head dangling almost between his knees, seemingly wishing he was dead. It seemed like the end of the world but it was just the end of the season. Branca recovered and went on to pitch four more years. He was traded to the American League, wound up briefly with the Yankees, but came back to Brooklyn to marry Ann Mulvey, younger daughter of the Mulveys, who owned a quarter of the club.

As explosive as was Thomson's memorable blow, equally dramatic was Don Larsen's sustained pitching which resulted in the only perfect game in World Series history. There have been a total of ten pitched. Larsen's was number 6. He performed the feat on a hazy October afternoon in the 1956 Yankee-Dodger series, the last one played where both ball parks were within the city limits.

The details of Larsen's ninety-seven pitches have been examined many times. The story of Dale Mitchell's half-swing at a final third strike with plate umpire Babe Pinelli ringing down the curtain on his own distinguished career with that big out has a lasting place in sports literature.

What isn't as well known, perhaps, is that Larsen had been Casey Stengel's choice to try to pull the Yankees back even after the Dodgers had chased Whitey Ford in the opener. So Larsen started game number two over in Ebbets Field before a capacity crowd of 36,217 and he failed to survive the second inning. The Yankees got him a six-run lead but it wasn't enough. Larsen was wild from the opening pitch and when he managed to find the plate the Dodgers hit him with enthusiasm.

Johnny Kucks, a youthful low-ball reliever, had to bail him out of the inning; then Kucks didn't prove much of an improvement. Duke Snider nailed him for a three-run homer in one of those bat-around innings and now the score was tied.

It didn't stay that way long. The Dodgers kept hitting and Casey Stengel kept sending in pitchers. At the end of a three-and-one-half-hour game the Dodgers had faced seven of them and collected thirteen runs, at that time the most ever given up by a Yankee team in a World Series. The Dodgers now also had a two to nothing lead in games.

Whitey Ford got things back on the track with a victory in game number three and Tom Sturdivant went the distance for another Yankee victory in game number four to tie it up.

Now it was up to Casey to decide on either Larsen or Bob Turley, the other pitcher who had come in that deal with Baltimore a couple of years earlier. He went with Larsen, and the Dodgers with Sal Maglie, who had been to Cleveland after he departed the Giants.

In any successful venture a certain amount of luck figures. It had better. Branch Rickey, in his annual speech to the rookies in spring training, used to call it the "residue of design," meaning that luck comes to those who plan ahead. Larsen could hardly be called a planner. His luck ran in the following fashion:

First, he had control. He struck out a comparatively modest total of seven, but on only one hitter did he go to a three-balls count.

There was a hair-raising recovery by Gil McDougald for a successful peg to first after Jackie Robinson had sent a rifle shot at Andy Carey. It came off Andy's glove and McDougald was on the ball like a cat in time for a successful throw to Joe Collins at first base. Not many of those, a third-to-short-to-first sequence.

In the fifth inning Mickey Mantle ran a mile for a backhanded catch on Gil Hodges and in the same inning there was a drive by little Sandy Amoros that curved into foul territory in right field, missing by no more than a foot.

That was really all the "luck" Larsen needed. He tried baffling the hitters with a new stance, one which he had adopted in the late stages of the pennant race. No wind-up. No one had told him to change. He claimed it came to him in one revealing flash while warming up before a winning game in Boston in early September.

It seemed to keep the hitters off balance, destroying the rhythm which was keyed to a pitcher's standard crank-up. Later Bob Turley adopted it; he had a big year in 1958 crowned by the Cy Young Award with a twenty-one and seven record.

Turley and Larsen came to the Yankees in a seven-player deal with Baltimore which was completed in stages after the 1954 season. The two big pitchers were not the only ones with memorable careers however. Among the seven coming from Baltimore (nine were sent in return by the Yankees) were two who went on to become major league managers in the seventies. They were Billy Hunter, a shortstop, and Darrell Johnson, a fine catcher with little hitting ability. Johnson stuck around as a third catcher with the Yankees a long time, picking up nuggets from Stengel and Ralph Houk, then moved along into a managing career which included a seven-game Series with the 1975 Red Sox against Cincinnati.

In the group dispatched by the Yankees were Willie Miranda, the handsome little Cuban shortstop who fielded as elegantly as Phil Rizzuto but was a powder-puff hitter, and Gene Woodling, a Series veteran. Being traded was nothing new for Willie Miranda. In 1952–53 he wore five different uniforms.

Frank Lane was running the Chicago White Sox and Bill Veeck was dying in St. Louis. When they wanted to get their minds off their dwindling box office receipts they'd call each other on the phone and trade Willie Miranda. Not just Willie, alone, but he'd always be in there in some two- or three-man deal.

Miranda started and ended the '52 season with the White Sox and was traded back to the Browns in the off season. In 1953 he was sold to the Yankees at the mid-June deadline and found himself on a world championship club. It was his first and only association with winners. As mentioned he was a dandy-looking fellow and could easily have qualified for Hollywood.

Incidentally, trading Willie around like an unregistered bond was completely legal. The railroads and the airlines applauded it, and every time he was traded a fee went to the American League office, so there was no complaint from the establishment. Miranda, meanwhile, wisely patronized only one-day laundry services during this interlude.

Larsen got incredible mileage out of his performance. He was still around in 1967, having been with seven other clubs, and he had a meager winning total of sixty-two games to show for those eleven seasons. Fortunately or unfortunately baseball front office people tend to become fans as much as their customers. How could you not take a chance on a fellow who had pitched a perfect game in the World Series?

Larsen's departure from the Yankees preceded that of Casey Stengel by one year. Stengel liked the big righthander and made allowances for his sometimes erratic lifestyle. The cops picked Larsen up in St. Petersburg one spring training season just as rosey-fingered dawn was starting to paint the sky above St. Petersburg Bay. Larsen had made his presence known to the cops with a loud crash which occurred as he was wrapping his car around a lamp post which just happened to be standing there.

Stengel was advised of this development at breakfast. Like a lot of old ball players his first meal of the day was a hearty one highlighted by plenty of bacon, sausages, and other heavy delicacies. Casey never missed a stroke as he learned his World Series hero-to-be had been in a car accident at 5 a.m. "Jeez," he said, "that's kind of early to go out and mail a letter."

Books have been written about spring training, the heart-break, the talent which bubbles to the top, and the nonsense. Sometimes newsmen figure in the proceedings. One of the better ones of the fifties, Jack Orr, was in a brief encounter which still brings a chuckle.

A west coaster originally and very strong for the rights-of-man, Jack worked for a couple of liberal losers in New York, Ralph Ingersoll's *PM*, the *Star* and the *Compass*, newspapers long since consigned to the dusty files. Later, Jack who liked to stay up late and look upon the wine when it was red, sent a record into the books by being fired from all three Philadelphia papers. He had lost an eye in a childhood accident, but it didn't bother his looking.

In a St. Pete bar one night he looked across at an attractive woman having a solo drink. Spring training seemed to be stretching forever; home was far, far away and it was probably snowing in New York anyway. Orr told the bartender to send a drink over to the lady.

Soon they were having an animated conversation. She knew something about both the Yankees and the Cardinals, who also trained in St. Pete and about a number of other topics, too. Then she observed, "You're not a baseball player. What do you do?"

"I'm a newspaperman," announced Jack, drawing himself up that extra inch or two.

"Oh," she said, "I have a son in the same business. You might know him. His name is Walter Cronkite."

14

Please Speak into the Mike

PRIOR TO THE FIFTIES TV was of scant importance to the baseball world. In 1949 NBC strung together a "network" and boasted it ran all the way from Schenectady, New York to Washington, D.C. It carried the World Series between the Yankees and the Dodgers and if the telecast was mentioned in any of the accounts of that Series it was somewhere near the notes about how many hot dogs had been consumed, and what time the gates would open the following day.

In those days there weren't enough TV sets around for anyone to worry about. The idea of a TV assignment as a possible future plum for any of the broadcasters would have been treated as some kind of a joke. Radio carried the heavy impact and of course the newspapers were at their absolute peak. A baseball writing job on any newspaper—that was the real plum. Young men cheated, lied, and under-cut for the privilege of covering baseball. Papers were relatively cheap, mostly a nickel week-days, fifteen cents Sundays. Rare was the sports fan satisfied

143

with only one version of a game involving his favorite team. Getting a second opinion via some other writer's column was standard.

The fifties changed the TV picture dramatically, beginning with that first coast-to-coast telecast of the National League's '51 playoff series between the Dodgers and the Giants. Later in the week the Yankees-Giants World Series went coast to coast and after that it seemed as though there had always been stuff on the tube taking place in Los Angeles seen in New York and vice versa.

As the decade rolled along TV's influence grew greater. By the sixties it had firmly established its claim as an equal with the print media as a means of bringing the game to the public, and in the seventies it pretty much took over the game.

As money poured into baseball from the networks in a deluge no one would have dreamed of, the owners needed no prodding to go along with anything their new "partners" suggested. A game in Los Angeles at 5 p.m. to accommodate the World Series viewers in the vital East in prime time? Fine. A divisional playoff in a pouring rain so that the programming the following day wouldn't be disrupted? No problem.

Between TV on one hand and players' salary demands on the other, only a village idiot couldn't see that the game would not remain in the hands of the men who own the franchises. The interesting part will come, as it must inevitably, when TV finds something more attractive, and cheaper, to program. Like elephants making love. In prime time, of course.

Baseball helped develop some of the most influential TV and radio sports personalities, men able to "deliver a market" in a manner guaranteed to bring joy to those concerned with cost-per-thousand. While they didn't have the impact of a Walter Winchell, or an Eddie Cantor, if you were an advertiser interested in reaching the millions interested in baseball in this era, there were several people who could help you do the job. Among them were Mel Allen in New York, Red Barber and Vin Scully in Brooklyn, Ernie Harwell in Baltimore and Detroit, and Harry Caray in St. Louis.

Followings were enormous. When Mel Allen was referred to within the inner sanctums of the advertising agencies as "the twenty-sixth Yankee" (the regular twenty-five-man roster, plus one) few dared laugh. He sold a lot of White Owl cigars and Ballantine beer.

Allen, an Alabaman whose regional accent became more pronounced in later years along with his total inability to turn off his one-way conversation, was the source from whence sprung another generation of baseball broadcasters. Working with Mel in New York doing the Yankees was virtually a guarantee you'd get the number one job in some other city. The list is long: Curt Gowdy went to Boston, Russ Hodges across the river to the New York Giants and later San Francisco, Jim Woods went to Pittsburgh, and Joe Garagiola later enjoyed all kinds of electronic fame and fortune as well as having a golf tournament named after him.

Allen had an unusually long run with the Yankees. He began before World War II, took time out for military service, and ran into the mid-sixties until he was unceremoniously yanked in the middle of a Yankees-Cards World Series. There was a Mel Allen cult, with people trying to imitate his "How about that?" In his mid-sixties Allen today commands a bigger hand at baseball gatherings than the stars whose exploits he recounted.

For a while the Yankees had a Mel Allen-Red Barber duo, which would be impossible to duplicate today. Barber had built a fervid following in Brooklyn after coming from Cincinnati with Larry MacPhail. Expressions like "sitting in the catbird seat," and "tearing up the old pea patch," plus one or two others, all delivered in a soft Southern-fried accent (he was a Floridian), had an odd ring when translated into the harsher accents of Brooklyn's two-million-plus population.

MacPhail's successor in running the Dodgers, Branch Rickey, was a great admirer of Barber's. (The Redhead was a lay preacher and Rickey was very strong with church-going tendencies, which extended to his refusal to attend ball games on Sunday.) When Rickey left, that connection didn't continue with the new boss, Walter O'Malley. According to Barber's account

O'Malley offered him five hundred dollars to do a World Series, which meant he either didn't want him or he was very broke. In any case Barber decided a move was in order and went over to the Yankees who were having a tough time filling that number two spot behind Mel.

For a while the Yankees had Dizzy Dean on the pre- and post-game shows but Dizzy's raw-bone humor failed to impress listeners in the number one market. His "slud into second" faded the second time around. Also, his telling of the exploits of the Gashouse Gang in St. Louis under Frank Frisch in the thirties, when dropping bags of water out of hotel windows was the height of fun and games, palled on the ears of sophisticated New Yorkers. Sure, he and his brother Paul almost pitched no-hitters on the same day over in Brooklyn (Paul did, and Dizzy had to be satisfied with a shutout.) but after that what else was new, Diz?

Eventually Dizzy reluctantly packed it in for a job on Game of the Week. His reluctance can be traced to the fact that with the Yankees he was practically able to live off his winnings playing golf with Dan Topping, one of the Yankee owners.

Dean presumably is telling those cotton-pickin' stories up there in the Great Dugout in the Skies but he did leave New York at least one good line.

He was in the booth at Yankee Stadium one night when a foul tip off Johnny Mize's mighty bat came whistling up and nailed the radio engineer right between the eyes. Back he toppled with an awful crash. There was a lot of scuffling audible on the air, then a moment's silence. Finally, Dean's voice chirped, "That one hit our engineer Lou right between the eyes. But if his wife or anyone else is listening, he's okay. Y'gotta be careful and stay alert for balls like that, though. When they come back and hit you in a spot like that they can really sting."

Joe DiMaggio had a brief fling as a TV announcer with the Yankees after he had turned down the club's offer of another $100,000 contract in 1952 even though everyone was aware of DiMaggio's excruciating arthritis. DiMaggio had insisted after 1951 that he wasn't going to embarrass himself or anyone else by trying to play with less than 100 percent efficiency.

DiMaggio disliked the TV role and was never at ease even though people fell all over themselves in an effort to help. He packed it in after a year, vowing never again. Ironically he had a second career—more lucrative than the one as a ball player— as a commercials personality hustling bank services and coffee makers.

A third Hall of Famer was prominent at the mike in the fifties and sixties. He was Waite Hoyt, a member of the Yankee club that dominated the game in the late twenties. They won successive World Series, four games to zip. Hoyt wound up in Cincinnati, rapidly became a household name and a force in the community. He taught a few million people in southern Ohio the finer points of the game.

Hoyt had an unusual delivery on the air. Everything was in the past tense. "The pitch was over the plate, Sauer cracked it to center where it was caught by Duke Snider. Two out." It took a little getting used to.

Hoyt's forceful personality, which sometimes teetered on the abrasive, also took a little getting used to, but once past that hurdle he proved one of the more delightful and informed people a young writer could hope to meet. He told Babe Ruth stories by the dozen (he ran at night with Ruth before he took the pledge) and he played for all three clubs in the New York area. His success, however, was with the Yankees and he never forgot it. It was late in his career when he was pitching for the Pirates during one of those seven-won, five-lost seasons, and the opposition was beginning to get on him. He took it just so long, then turned to the offending dugout and snarled, "Shut up you guys or I'll put on a Yankee uniform and scare the shit out of all of you." A hushed silence followed.

Hoyt got the good Yankee dollar for his time as a headliner. (He got $11,000 in his twenty-two and seven season in '27, plus a small bonus for going past twenty.) Even though he was gone from the game long before the lunacy of quarter-million yearly salaries for .290 hitters or twelve-game winners, he found it difficult to relate to the six-figure salaries some of the stars got in the late sixties. He was fond of telling the story of his signing with the New York Giants as a schoolboy whiz out of Erasmus Hall High School in Brooklyn. It took him a half day to come over from that section of Brooklyn to the Giants' offices in downtown New York.

"I had to bring my father along to sign the contract," he recalled, "because I was a minor. To make the contract legal money had to change hands. So McGraw handed me a five-dollar bill like you'd give a kid a Christmas present.

"I stuck it into my pocket, thanked him, and we left. We walked down the stairs to the street where my father turned to me and said, 'Let's have the five.'"

Vin Scully was a child of the fifties, strongly favored by his Dodger boss, Walter O'Malley. This connection resulted in ultimate prosperity undreamt of when Scully was a Fordham University undergraduate and centerfielder.

Red Barber gave Scully his first break but it was in football, not baseball. CBS used to do a Saturday roundup of college football games with Barber handling all the reports flowing into New York. He'd check with a half-dozen men covering games around the country and bring them in for pieces of their action. It was called Sports Central or Radio Central or some similar original handle.

Scully was sent to Boston for a Clemson-Boston College game in old Braves Field where the accommodations for broadcasters were a notch below primitive. He and his lone engineer prowled the ice-covered roof of the old ball park peering down at the tiny figures while Scully's fingers froze to the mike.

In the flush of enthusiasm for his first assignment Scully had scorned a topcoat. He wore nothing but a sports jacket against the blasts coming off the neighboring Charles River.

Despite the obstacles Scully did an excellent job and Barber remembered. It made such an impression that when a spot opened in Brooklyn when Harwell left for the Giants, Barber thought of this young man. Scully went on to become one of the titans of TV sportscasting.

O'Malley's patronage helped, just as the kings and earls helped English painters like Reynolds, Gainsborough, Turner, and Constable. When the Dodgers went to the West Coast and O'Malley sold the first ten years of radio rights to Union Oil, a stipulation was made that Scully went along with the package. And Scully paid it back with unremitting loyalty.

Harwell's story has a few unusual overtones worth recalling. A long-time student of the game, he had advanced to broadcasting the Atlanta Crackers games when an emergency occurred in Brooklyn; Barber had a sudden attack of ulcers. The attack wiped him out of the '48 Olympics and left a gaping hole in the radio booth at Ebbets Field. Rickey had a good relationship with Earl Mann, who ran the Atlanta club, and asked for Harwell. Mann said, "Fine, but you have a catcher we want, Cliff Dapper."

Brooklyn had all the catching it needed for a foreseeable future with Roy Campanella, Bruce Edwards, Gil Hodges (recently switched to first base), Ferrell Anderson, and a half-dozen other aspirants spread among its two dozen farm clubs. So Harwell went into the record book as the only baseball announcer ever traded for a catcher.

They did things like that in the Southern Association. Joe Engel, owner at Chattanooga, once traded a player for a turkey at Thanksgiving. His excellent premise was that a turkey was less difficult to clean than a ball player.

Just as in football, baseball has come to call upon ex-players in increasing numbers for radio and TV. There's Phil Rizzuto, a Yankee star under Joe McCarthy and later Casey Stengel, who has been broadcasting for his old club for more than two decades; there's George Kell, like Rizzuto, of Hall of Fame stature, working in Detroit; there's Don Drysdale, a two-hundred-game winner for the Dodgers working for the Angels; there's Maury Wills, Tony Kubek, and Joe Garagiola with NBC; there's Lou Boudreau in Chicago; Richie Ashburn in Philadelphia; Ralph Kiner with the New York Mets; Mike Shannon with St. Louis; Jerry Coleman with San Diego; Ernie Johnson with

Atlanta; Jim Piersall with the White Sox; Herb Score in Cleveland; and Bill White, the old first baseman with the Yankees.

It would seem a pretty good idea for a doting father when he buys that $30 glove for his kid for Little League that he invest another ten bucks for a good dictionary for the young man.

15

Hold the Presses

THERE WERE THREE MAJOR WIRE SERVICES in the fifties instead
of the current two. The Associated Press and United Press were
the heavyweights, with the International News Service bringing
up the rear. INS had its anchor in the diminishing number of
papers in the Hearst empire, at one time the most potent in the
country. Eventually INS merged with the United Press to
become UPI. That logo may be seen in today's newspapers.

All three went in hot and heavy for sports coverage, with the
emphasis on baseball. Pro football was just struggling to meet
the payroll; there was no big-league soccer; pro basketball
players in the fledgling NBA were getting a couple hundred
bucks a game, and so were the Canadian farm kids, with one or
two exceptions. The National Hockey League, which wasn't
really national at all, had a couple of Canadian clubs and had
four more in the upper-right quadrant of this country (Detroit,
Chicago, Boston, and New York). Pro tennis was non-existent—
the only way to make a living in tennis was to stay amateur

and take the pittance under the table. The golfers were starting to show some signs of life, but still a lot of prizes were redeemable down at the supermarket or at a participating gas station.

The big job on the wire services, as with the daily papers, was baseball. Those assigned didn't dare complain about working long, sometimes strange, hours. The second time they'd complain there'd be a fresh, eager face in there to gather up the stray pearls strewn around the clubhouse floor.

One of INS's baseball writers was Charley Einstein, introduced to us early as the ghost of Willie Mays. Einstein could not only write swiftly and well but didn't mind a summons at an off-hour. Lawton Carver, his boss, was a typical old-line newspaperman. Clocks meant nothing, and the saloons in New York stayed open until four in the morning.

Now it's late and the Yankees and the Orioles pull off a trade of considerable magnitude. It obviously means the wrap-up of another pennant for the Yankees if it all works out. (Since it was the Bob Turley-Don Larsen deal, it did.)

The news breaks out of Baltimore, but the INS man down there can't do much more than provide the bare facts. Someone around New York has to go chase the Yankees' general manager, George Weiss, who is supposed to be up at his home in Connecticut but who is actually hiding from reporters in a New York hotel.

Carver grabs the phone and snaps, "Get me Einstein."

The switchboard operator had her pick of two Einsteins, and, you guessed it. The phone rang in the library of the man who had worked out the theory of relativity and the earth-shaking equation $E=mc^2$. Carver picked up the phone on the other end and started explaining about the big trade, what was needed in a hurry, and that maybe Charley ought to hop in a cab and get his ass over to the office in about fifteen minutes flat.

The man on the other end was definitely interested and wanted to discuss the problem further. "Look Charley," snapped Carver, "I don't want to fool around with any of your goddam vaudeville routines." (Einstein's father had been Parkykarkuss, a Greek comedian who had played alongside Eddie Cantor on

Sunday night radio.) "Those other sons-a-bitches probably have the whole story wrapped up by now." He slammed the receiver and turned to a nearby dandruff-scratcher on the copy desk and announced, "That goddam Einstein's drunk."

An hour later, with Charley still missing, Carver put in another call. There was another operator on and this one figured when the sports department wanted an Einstein it didn't want to talk about quantum physics. Charley got on the phone and listened to five minutes of unremitting raving.

A you-never-called-me would definitely have been the wrong answer. Quick to sense the emergency involved, Charley soothed, "Be there in ten minutes, boss." He threw his coat on and said to his wife, "There's some kind of a big baseball story breaking. It's going to be a tough night. Carver is drunk."

Baseball and whiskey don't mix, especially with third basemen who have to move up on a possible bunt by a .300 slugger. Baseball writing and whiskey don't go together too well either, although some of the better legends usually have Johnny Walker overtones. F'rinstance in the matter of keeping score, an absolute requirement in the industry. An aspirant for a baseball writer's job rarely learns the shorthand which tracks hitters around the bases by practicing on the job. He's probably already learned it playing for the Good News Bears in Little League.

There's a numbering system used which is as old as major league baseball itself, invented by a baseball writer on the old *New Yord Herald* named Mike Kelly. Kelly assigned numbers to each position and they're still in use: one for the pitcher, two for the catcher, three for first base, four for second, five for third, six for short, seven for left field, eight for center, and nine for right. This, plus a handful of other cabalistic tracings is the basic material.

It was such a perfect system that there's been little success by those trying to improve on it over a century. It used to give me a little chill when I realized I was using the same kind of shorthand as baseball writers who had served as war correspondents at Gettysburg and Shiloh.

Kelly is remembered by the symbol for a strikeout, *K*. The

letter faces the normal way when a batter swings at a third strike, and is turned facing the other way when he looks at one. Marvelous.

This universal scoring system has been of untold value to those covering the game. When a writer says to his cohorts, "Catch me up, chum," meaning "I'm late, or I've fallen behind, or I was on the phone; please fill me in on the details up to this moment," there is no problem.

Only the most intricate of plays will require more than a few seconds. Mostly it's a quick litany of numbers delivered as fast as the catcher-up can move his pencil.

Some writers, naturally, are more diligent than others. In the fifties the writers always seemed to be missing a train and arriving in the middle of a game. Or on the road they'd miss the elevator back at the hotel and decide to go back to the room for a few extras. As long as you made it to the park before that final out there was nothing to worry about. The code of comradery, baseball writers' style, ruled out turning anyone down in the catch-me-up category.

Hilarious overtones have been known to reep into the picture. One evening in Los Angeles one of the local writers who had gained the proud distinction of never having spilled a drop managed to get to the press box. He flopped down alongside a companion, managed a feeble smile and uttered the rallying cry of the clan, "Catch me up, chum."

Dutifully the other started to rattle off names and numbers, "Gilliam pop four (popped up to the second baseman); Neal bunt two to three (thrown out by the catcher while attempting to bunt); Moon line single eight (Moon singled to center); Larker look (Larker took a third strike)." And so it went.

Then he gave the other side and, rattling along, came to a play which had impressed him more than most he had witnessed recently. "Groat slapped one down to Wills who made a great play. He grabbed it underhand, barehanded, and got it to third ahead of the runner. Really, a great play, Frank?" And he started to go on, only to become aware that his listener had stopped and was staring at him, pencil poised.

"Whatsamatter, Frank?" he asked.

"That great play," said the writer with all the dignity he could muster, "Let me be the judge of it."

Physically and psychologically, the baseball press boxes changed in the fifties. With the switching around of franchises writers found themselves in unfamiliar surroundings. Baltimore, Milwaukee, Kansas City, Los Angeles, San Francisco. For some of those with habits difficult to rework it was a period of trial. Where's the pencil sharpener? Where's the men's room?

A fresh breeze blew through these preferred seats, high above home plate. As the guard changed baseball writers who had seemed to enjoy a permanent grip on the job since John McGraw and Miller Huggins were managers suddenly found the climb to some of the crow's nests a little too much. They either packed it in entirely or went inside to the copy desk to push a pencil across young people's stuff.

Others couldn't take the switch to night games. The most famous observation in this connection came from Edward T. Murphy, a long-time baseball writer with the *New York Sun*. Murphy covered Brooklyn in the days of the Daffiness Boys and he came up with the line, "Over-confidence may cost the Dodgers seventh place." Better still was his quote on night baseball when he quit, saying, "I'm not going to sit around all day like a burglar waiting for it to get dark so I can go to work."

The new people were younger, of course. With their new attitudes they preferred to quote a live Mickey Mantle or a Don Newcombe rather than a dead Honus Wagner or a Three-Finger Brown. They were properly respectful of their elders and listened to the tales of the Babe's sexual prowess ("He counted 'em by the number of cigar butts he left on the window sill during the night.") or about the time the Gashouse Gang from St. Louis dressed up like carpenters and disrupted a ladies society lunch in a hotel in Philadelphia. Sure, sure, they said, and then they'd go off and talk with Casey Stengel who was in the process of winning five straight World Series, or put it to Leo Durocher, "C'mon Leo, would you really throw at your grandmother?"

The older press boxes in places like Boston, New York, St.

Louis, Chicago, and Detroit, were bastions in an era of change. There always seemed to be that same fellow at the gate or handing you a scorecard. Five years might have passed in the other league, but when you got back these fellows had never changed. Even the women dishing out the sandwiches had that built-in look, along with the Western Union personnel.

The new writers usually were fresh out of either World War II or Korea. Some had developed an awareness about things other than hitting for the cycle (single, double, triple and homer in the same game, and how about that, folks?). One-hit pitching performances paled a little beside what was going on down in Washington where Joe McCarthy was scaring Eisenhower fifty times as badly as the Nazi hordes had scared him as Supreme Commander of the Allies.

The writing was different, too. Sometimes they wrote the way jazz musicians played. The theme was always there but the variations were dazzling and sometimes a little disconcerting. Like the time there was an addition to a pitcher's family and the player was handing out cigars and accepting congratulations and yes, yes, Barbara was fine.

What was she doing? (Meaning, was she at home watching him pitch that day?) "I guess she's home feeding the baby," he replied.

"Breast or bottle?" was the next query. Things like that.

Jimmy Cannon, an outstanding columnist for four decades, was of the older group, but he was still able to move pretty fast and to compete. He disliked these new antics. "Jeez," he stormed, "they get something and they go off in a corner and they toss it around amongst themselves like a lot of chipmunks. That's what they are, a bunch of chipmunks. We ought to organize and protect ourselves. Let's call ourselves the 'vigilantes.'"

"Vigilantes" faded in a hurry but the tag "chipmunk" stuck. Today there are writers pushing fifty who say with a kind of pride, "I was a chipmunk." Some even have that overbite to prove it.

For almost a half-century, covering baseball was highly formalized. If you worked for a morning paper you wrote about what happened on the field. You entered the press box when the game began and when you left it your day's chore was done. The locker room, with the quotes and reactions, was strictly the province of the writers for the afternoon papers. (There were a lot more of them than there are today.)

Youthful enterprise plus the pressure of TV changed all that. TV showed anyone who was interested exactly what was going on down on the field. Later, with instant replay, they were able to show it more than once, putting the writer at a disadvantage with his one shot at it. But one day, someone thought to ask the management to install a TV set in the press box.

So the morning papers, despite the pressure of early deadlines, found themselves down in the clubhouse after a game, asking questions ("What kind of a pitch did you get Kaline on in the ninth?" "Were you upset when the Old Man took you out?" and so forth). Afternoon writers glared at the incursion, but it was a free country. Today, quotes are a vital part of all baseball accounts, morning and afternoon. In the old days stories in the morning papers usually were blocks of solid type, unrelieved by quotation marks.

The baseball writers were the first to organize in the sports-writing field. Today theirs is still the best professional group as far as control of working conditions is concerned.

It was formed because the owners showed scant regard for the men who were providing them with thousands of dollars of free publicity. To show how scant it was they'd give away seats in the press box to politicians, saloon keepers, and sundry friends. Since the first decade of this century a million actors have trod the boards. Louis Mann, a friend of John McGraw, even watched a game with a writer seated in his lap. McGraw had given Mann the writer's seat. A Chicagoan following the Cubs, Hugh Fullerton wasn't going to stand through the game. Later he was a founder of the Baseball Writers Association. Today the writers control the press boxes, the scoring, accredit writers to the limited space at World Series, and pay an occasional funeral expense for one of the brothers whose luck has run out or who has lived too long.

The stipulations are pretty much the same for membership as they were when it was first organized sixty years ago. You must cover baseball as a full-time assignment for a daily paper. To serve as an official scorer off a rotating list you must cover a hundred games a year for at least three years. The fee is a modest one, fifty dollars, and it's a bargain for baseball because to hire rotating scorers who would travel like umpires (otherwise you'd have the customers complaining about home-town calls) would cost ten times that amount. Occasionally writers have taken themselves off the list when players get a little too hot about a hit or error call.

There is a tradition of baseball writers helping each other. A new man shows up, and an older one takes him around and introduces him to those with whom he'll have daily contact. A writer doesn't show for one of several well-worn reasons on the road and someone will cover for him.

This used to be an easy matter when everything went Western Union. The only detail which required attention was making sure not more than one story was filed by the Samaritans to the erring scribe's paper. With telephone communication today and things like dictation, etc., it's a lot tougher. The new telecopier system, where a sheet of manuscript is transmitted exactly as typed over a telephone via a whirring cylinder, may restore this brotherly arrangement.

The press box was, and remains, the command post for the media at a ball park, but no area can be ruled out as one where news can develop: the dugouts before the game, the clubhouses after, the hotel lobbies where the teams stay, the busses hauling the gladiators to and from the field, the planes whizzing from one city to the next. Everywhere the team goes reporters must follow, lugging their suitcases, portable typewriters, telecopiers, and something picked up in Cincinnati for the little lady.

Which leads to the story about one baseball writer's wife complaining to her husband that he wasn't particularly thoughtful. Phil, one of her husband's colleagues, was always bringing his wife something. "How come," she complained, "you don't bring me anything when you come off the road?"

"I don't know," replied the husband, "I guess you're just lucky."

A lot of people rate baseball writing a gold-plated pass through life. Watching baseball games can hardly be called work among people who have to cheat every day in real estate, or sell tires, or razzle-dazzle some oldster with the provisions of an insurance policy. They look, and they envy.

From an old scorebook I came up with the following scribbled in the back, "What they say to Yankee writers." These are the questions. With a change of a name or two writers today probably still hear them, if they care to listen:

1. You mean all you have to do is just watch a ball game?
2. You must get through real early. What do you do with your time (leer, here)?
3. What kind of a guy is Casey Stengel? Really.
4. How much of a cut do you get from the World Series?
5. It must be great knowing guys like Mickey, Whitey, and Yogi, huh?
6. Is Mickey Mantle really married and what does his wife say?
7. Are the ball players really chased by all those broads and do you get any that's left over?
8. They tell me the ball club wines and dines you writers every night.
9. You can get as many passes as you want, can't you?

The adversary role of newsman vs. ball player-manager-coach was just as strong in the fifties as it is today. But the newsman seeking out information the other side would just as soon conceal is at a considerable disadvantage today compared to twenty years ago. TV has poured millions into baseball and the establishment thinking is that a hundred years of free publicity was fine, but have you had a look at the figures on the last check from television? God help baseball if that thinking is ever put to the ultimate test.

In TV they change programming (and baseball is programming just as much as an ethnic situation-comedy) the way the executives change wives and the middle-management people change underwear. In contrast, some American newspapers claim they reported the results of the Alexander Hamilton-Aaron Burr duel.

I have heard managers curse out newspapermen in language you wouldn't use on a child molester just to make a quick, cheap impression on their grinning players. I have also heard players abuse newspapermen unspeakably over the national-security matter of a scoring judgment on a base hit or an error. But nothing much will change until TV's golden showers terminate.

Owners should remember that just as cheap, easy programming attracted TV to the national pastime, so something else can come along to turn their pointy heads completely as they shoot for the lowest common denominator and the highest ratings. How about elephants getting together in mating season? What chance would the World Series have against that on the tube?

On a more pleasant, less self-serving note, there have been gentlemen on both sides, and still are. PeeWee Reese used to say, "When I have a bad day I just don't read the papers the next day," and let it go at that while people like Jackie Robinson screamed and Duke Snider sulked.

For every time Leo Durocher cursed and threatened ("I could sue the bastard and his paper for two million but I'm too nice a guy."), there was a Stengel who would take a newsman aside and suggest that if he looked for such-and-such on a particular play he'd have a better understanding of it. For all the Ted Williamses spitting on newsmen (and fans—he was once fined five thousand dollars for this little caper) there were the Stan Musials asking about the family.

And there was Grantland Rice at the end of the early fifties, finishing up in the press box where he had started. Rice was a true titan, a former athlete, a poet, and a writer who had made a lot of money and had enjoyed spending it.

In the thirties and forties Rice was the biggest name in sports, frequently transcending the material he wrote about. His *Sportlight* newsreel was seen in thousands of movie houses every week; his syndicated column was carried in hundreds of papers. Granny's cachet on any project meant its instant success. He was a big man but he stooped to praise kid reporters, remembering perhaps some particular line they had written, thereby becoming forever a part of their memories.

Like everything else put on earth Grantland Rice had a definite time frame. It had passed in the fifties. Newsreels were made obsolete by nightly TV newscasts; his syndicated column was now being carried purely as a favor by a few trusted friends spotted around the country. Other writers, other styles had come along.

The luck of the seating plan put Grantland Rice in the seat next to me at Yankee Stadium during the first four Series of the fifties. All involved the Yankees vs. the Phillies, the Giants, and a couple with the Dodgers. Each year he would haul a large, old-fashioned portable out after the game and start pecking away just as he had done when describing the Four Horsemen in the twenties, the Gashouse Gang and Babe Ruth in the thirties, and the Chicago Bears and Joe Louis in the forties.

That was my last picture of Grantland Rice. The last game of the Series was over and everyone was busy getting set to commit the day's doings to unperishable prose. Out came Grantland Rice's typewriter, its owner being careful not to bump the nearby occupants of the crowded seats with his still-stalwart shoulders. He slipped a single sheet in the roller and typed, "By Grantland Rice," and on the next line, "Special to the *Winnipeg Star.*"

The last surviving outpost of his once formidable journalistic empire wasn't even within the borders of the United States.

Baseball Records in the Fifties

Year	American League Winner	National League Winner	World Series	American League Batting	National League Batting
1950	New York	Philadelphia	New York, 4–0	Billy Goodman, Boston, .354	Stan Musial, St. Louis, .346
1951	New York	New York	New York, 4–2	Ferris Fain, Philadelphia, .344	Stan Musial, St. Louis, .355
1952	New York	Brooklyn	New York, 4–3	Ferris Fain, Philadelphia, .327	Stan Musial, St. Louis, .326
1953	New York	Brooklyn	New York, 4–2	Mickey Vernon, Washington, .337	Carl Furillo, Brooklyn, .344
1954	Cleveland	New York	New York, 4–0	Bob Avila, Cleveland, .341	Willie Mays, New York, .345
1955	New York	Brooklyn	Brooklyn, 4–3	Al Kaline, Detroit, .340	Richie Ashburn, Philadelphia, .338
1956	New York	Brooklyn	New York, 4–3	Mickey Mantle, New York, .353	Hank Aaron, Milwaukee, .328
1957	New York	Milwaukee	Milwaukee, 4–3	Ted Williams, Boston, .388	Stan Musial, St. Louis, .351
1958	New York	Milwaukee	New York, 4–3	Ted Williams, Boston, .328	Richie Ashburn, Philadelphia, .350
1959	Chicago	Los Angeles	Los Angeles, 4–2	Harvey Kuenn, Detroit, .353	Hank Aaron, Milwaukee, .355

Year	*American League Pitching (W-L)*	*National League Pitching (W-L)*	*American League MVP*	*National League MVP*
1950	Vic Raschi, New York, .724 (21–8)	Sal Maglie, New York, .818 (18–4)	Phil Rizzuto, New York	Jim Konstanty, Philadelphia
1951	Bob Feller, Cleveland, .733 (22–8) Morrie Martin, Philadelphia, .733 (11–4)	Preacher Roe, Brooklyn, .880 (22–3)	Yogi Berra, New York	Roy Campanella, Brooklyn
1952	Bob Shantz, Philadelphia, .774 (24–7)	Hoyt Wilhelm, New York, .833 (15–3)	Bob Shantz, Philadelphia	Hank Sauer, Chicago
1953	Ed Lopat, New York, .800 (16–4)	Carl Erskine, Brooklyn, .769 (20–6)	Al Rosen, Cleveland	Roy Campanella, Brooklyn
1954	Sandy Consuegra, Chicago, .842 (16–3)	John Antonelli, New York, .750 (21–7) Hoyt Wilhelm, New York, .750 (12–4)	Yogi Berra, New York	Willie Mays, New York
1955	Tommy Byrne, New York, .762 (16–5)	Don Newcombe, Brooklyn, .800 (20–5)	Yogi Berra, New York	Roy Campanella, Brooklyn
1956	Whitey Ford, New York, .760 (19–6)	Don Newcombe, Brooklyn, .794 (27–7)	Mickey Mantle, New York	Don Newcombe, Brooklyn
1957	Tom Sturdivant, New York, .727 (16–6) Dick Donovan, Chicago, .727 (16–6)	Bob Buhl, Milwaukee, .720 (18–7)	Mickey Mantle, New York	Hank Aaron, Milwaukee
1958	Bob Turley, New York, .750 (21–7)	Warren Spahn, Milwaukee, .667 (22–11) Lew Burdette, Milwaukee, .667 (20–10)	Jack Jensen, Boston	Ernie Banks, Chicago
1959	Bob Shaw, Chicago, .750 (18–6)	Elroy Face, Pittsburgh, .947 (18–1)	Nellie Fox, Chicago	Ernie Banks, Chicago

INDEX